LOST
Wilderness in the

LOST in the Wilderness

FAITH PARKER

TATE PUBLISHING
AND ENTERPRISES, LLC

Lost in the Wilderness
Copyright © 2016 by Faith Parker. All rights reserved.

No part of this publication may be reproduced, stored in a retrieval system or transmitted in any way by any means, electronic, mechanical, photocopy, recording or otherwise without the prior permission of the author except as provided by USA copyright law.

This book is designed to provide accurate and authoritative information with regard to the subject matter covered. This information is given with the understanding that neither the author nor Tate Publishing, LLC is engaged in rendering legal, professional advice. Since the details of your situation are fact dependent, you should additionally seek the services of a competent professional.

The opinions expressed by the author are not necessarily those of Tate Publishing, LLC.

Published by Tate Publishing & Enterprises, LLC
127 E. Trade Center Terrace | Mustang, Oklahoma 73064 USA
1.888.361.9473 | www.tatepublishing.com

Tate Publishing is committed to excellence in the publishing industry. The company reflects the philosophy established by the founders, based on Psalm 68:11,
"The Lord gave the word and great was the company of those who published it."

Book design copyright © 2016 by Tate Publishing, LLC. All rights reserved.
Cover design by Joana Quilantang
Interior design by Jomar Ouano

Published in the United States of America
ISBN: 978-1-68237-905-9
1. Religion / Christian Life / Inspirational
2. Religion / Christian Life / Spiritual Growth
16.05.04

In loving memory of my father, Robert Quackenbos Sr.

Contents

Introduction 9

1	Reflecting	11
2	Honoring My Father	18
3	The Wilderness	22
4	Change Begins	40
5	A New Direction	51
6	Following Instructions	63
7	Prayer in the Wilderness	72
8	Fasting in the Wilderness	78
9	The Treasure Chest	84
10	The Narrow Path	98
11	Truths Revealed	112
12	"Do You Love Me?"	117
13	A Father's Love	126

Introduction

My father was someone I looked up to every day of my life. He was always there for me even when I didn't realize it. He touched my wounds and would give them a gentle kiss to take away the pain. He loved me more than my mind could ever imagine. My father would wrap his arms of love around me every time I was hurting or just needed the comfort of his love. My father guided me, directing me to live a life serving the risen Savior, and always encouraged me to reach for the stars. He held my hand when I was weak. He lifted me up when I could not walk. He sheltered me under the loving arms of his comfort and care. He touched my life in more ways than anyone could imagine. He always set the right example even when I would not follow his leading. He would hold my picture up and show it to everyone. Then he would brag and say, "This is my lovely daughter; I am so proud of her." My father loved me when I didn't even love myself. He knew my potential and knew God had a divine plan for my life. He taught me to always challenge myself and set goals so I had a direction in life. My father was a well-respected man, and many people knew him for the true person he was. My father taught me that even though the road is not always easy, I should trust that I will have the strength to follow through with my calling in life. He would tell me that if I would listen to the still, quiet voice and follow God's directions, I would be blessed. I dearly love my father, and I will never forget all the kind and comforting words he said to me. He saw value in each of his children, and he always had the right words to say if I would only listen and obey. I had to learn a lot for myself the hard way, but he always gave me the space to grow and let me learn from my mistakes.

The love and direction of a father is very important for the well-being of a child. Many children never get the opportunity to experience this love and guidance. Fortunately, I had a father who loved me and supplied the proper guidance throughout my life. My father knew the importance of being a godly man and setting the right example. A father has the responsibility of leading by example and guiding his children. Many fathers fail to give the most important treasures and gifts to their children, making it difficult to understand how precious these same gifts are when given by the Heavenly Father.

This book is a personal journey that began in late 2005. After the death of my father, I felt like I was lost in the wilderness. But my Heavenly Father was sitting at the potter's wheel. He was changing this broken vessel of clay. He had to take my heart and transform it to a heart desperately seeking after Him. He started transforming my mind to focus more on Him rather than on things of this world. He developed a thirst in me water would not satisfy. The more I began hearing the voice of God, the more He spoke to me. I had no idea what to expect next as God started to unfold right before my eyes His desires for my life. He was asking for sacrifices and change but allowed me to make the choices.

After being restored to an intimate relationship with God, I moved forward with new commitments and new challenges without knowing where the journey would take me. In this book, you will have the opportunity to read personal and intimate encounters I experienced with the Heavenly Father as He stood by my side, nurtured me, taught me, and guided me every step of the way. He was developing a disciple for Him. The journey brought back many memories of the dedication of my father and how he planted seeds to make me a woman after the heart of God. As I walked day by day seeking the face of God, I learned to value the treasures and gifts He offered. I gained new insight and strength to walk by faith and to share with others the gifts He gave me. I gained a deeper respect for my Heavenly Father as our relationship blossomed.

1
Reflecting

The birth of a baby girl named Faith was announced on November 19, 1958, in Sarasota, Florida, to Robert and Phyllis. I became the seventh and last child born to the family. I had five older brothers and one older sister. Born to parents in love with the Lord and a father who was a pastor, I had the opportunity to grow up in a Christian home. Even before birth, I was introduced to Jesus and attended church. As a family, we had devotions almost every evening, and we always prayed together. I had to memorize a Bible verse to recite to my parents daily, and my father would tell us Bible stories on a level that made them exciting and interesting to a child. I always wanted the attention of my father as I was Daddy's little girl. I can remember sitting on his lap and cuddling up in his masculine arms, feeling safe and secure. I knew the arms around me would protect me and defend me no matter what type of situation I encountered. I could just feel the love flowing out of his innermost being. I was fortunate to have the kind of father every child dreams of and deserves to have. There was always a feeling of comfort and peace living in the house with my father.

I remember striving to make my father proud of me in everything I set out to do. In school I wanted to get good grades so my father would be proud of me, and at home I wanted to be obedient to please him. As a teenager I remember putting pressure on myself to avoid making mistakes so I would not disappoint my father. I wanted to please my father in every way so I could see the delight in his face when he would talk about me to anyone.

When it came time to get married and leave home, my father struggled with letting me go. Our closeness was a bond that made it difficult for either of us to put distance between us. He cried at my wedding, and I knew it would take quite some time for him to get used to my not being around every day. Struggling, he let go little by little until he reached a comfort zone without ever turning completely loose. I knew my father and I would be close forever.

Although I was a blend of both of my parents, I had a lot of my father's personality. We were both aggressive at pursuing anything we decided to do—and doing it with perfection. Both of us were business-minded and set high standards for ourselves. I could pick up the phone and ask his advice on any situation I was facing in life. He always would give his advice, sit back, and let me make the final decisions. He never forced any of his opinions on me; he just let me know how he felt and what he thought was best. He let me learn from my mistakes and never threw them back in my face. With every mistake I made, he merely said, "Don't let it get the best of you; just let it be a lesson for you." Communication with one another was not a problem. I would listen and hear everything he was saying even if I did not agree. And my father always listened to what I had to say.

My father always stuck by me and encouraged me to be everything God wanted me to be. He would say, "Dream big." He would pray with me over any and every issue I faced in life. I could pick up the phone any time—day or night—and he was ready to pray with me. After our conversations, he would say, "Let's take it to the Lord in prayer," or "let your mother and me pray with you before hanging up the phone." I did not pay attention to his consistency and the importance the prayers played in my life until much later.

In late 2003, I received a call informing me my father was diagnosed with mesothelioma and was told that he had less than six months to live. I thought my world was caving in on me. How could I live without my father? He was always there for me. Now what would I do? Could this be a mistake? Surely my father would not die this young. Why was God allowing a man who loved and served Him to die? The same questions go through the mind of almost anyone getting this type of news. It takes a little while for reality to sink in and for someone to accept it is all part of God's plan—a part of life we have a hard time understanding.

The next year was not an easy one. My father started chemotherapy and was sick most of the time for the next six months. Any time spent with him was extremely hard on me as I watched his manly body start to become frail. At this point, I was glad he was still alive. The doctors were wrong about the six months. When six chemotherapy treatments were finished, testing proved the cancer was not in remission, and there was no need to do anything further. My heart sank again, and I knew time with my father was coming to an end. I continued to pray for my father, asking God for a miraculous healing, but in my heart I felt I would lose him before the end of 2004. After months of denial, I finally accepted that my father was not going to live much longer here on earth. God was taking him home to be with Him.

I wanted my father to leave Florida and come home with me so I could enjoy every minute I possibly could with him. I talked with my parents, and they decided they would come to North Carolina and live with me during the last months of his life. With nothing more the doctors could do, it was time to enjoy the last days with my father and help make him comfortable.

Struggling with leaving his own home and the comfort of his doctors, my father could never get to the point of saying he was ready to make the move. I made several trips to Florida to spend time with him. During my trip in early November, he said he wanted to pray a final prayer—a blessing for each of his children before he died. My father referenced back to the Old Testament where it was tradition for a father to pray and pass a blessing on to his children. If there was a blessing to be received after my father's death, he did not want me to miss out on it. Being obedient to God until the last moment of his life was still his goal.

I will never forget that day. I wondered if this would be the last time I would hear my father outwardly pray for me. I wished I could think of everything I wanted him to pray during the rest of my life so I could hear it spoken in this prayer. If I only had time to make a list, I am sure it would have had no end. I found comfort in my father's prayers, and I knew I would miss them. He was able to speak with God in a way I felt I never quite experienced in my personal prayer life. While growing up, I thought he had a special connection and a direct line through Jesus Christ straight to the heavenly Father.

Before leaving, he prayed for many things. He prayed for God to restore the joy I once had in Him. He asked God to show me His purpose and plan for my life and for me to willingly move into a new future with Him. My father asked God to bless my family and me in every way and to bless my business. He also prayed for many other things. With authority, he spoke some of the most beautiful words I had ever heard spoken. His prayer echoed in my mind for a long time as I left Florida. I headed back to North Carolina to take care of some business matters, knowing I would be back very soon.

My head was flooding with childhood memories as I started the eleven-hour trip back to North Carolina. I listened to a gospel CD, and every song that played brought back a memory of a time in my life when I heard my father's voice singing it. He would often sing hymns as we rode around in the car or as he worked around the house. Crying for over an hour, I just let his voice echo the words in my head. Then I jotted down the exact memory each song brought back into my mind—memories which had escaped from my mind for years, memories deeply hidden that brought to light what can never be replaced. I wanted to turn around and go back and just sit by my father's side until he took his last breath. I wanted to reminisce in his arms.

The next day I took time to write my father a letter sharing the memories I jotted down in my notebook. While writing this book, I began to search through all the documents on my computer, and this letter was one document I never deleted from my files. This was the last letter I wrote to my dad.

Dear Dad,

After leaving your home and getting several hours down the road, Jerry and I were listening to a gospel CD that we have. As I listened to the songs, I could still hear you and Mom singing the words to many of these songs like you did when I was a child. Back then I didn't realized how wonderful it sounded. To a kid, it was just singing, but now today, it has different memories. The echo of the words planted many seeds that make me the sensitive adult that I am today. Gospel music always stirs me up inside.

"Amazing Grace" was the first one that came on, and it was as though I heard you and Mom harmonizing instead of the singers on the CD. God's grace is truly amazing! Thanks for the Christian leadership and for helping me to always see God's amazing grace.

Then I listened to the song "Love lifted Me," and I thought of how many times love did lift me out of the pain, hurt, sin—you name it. I realize that again I will need God's love to lift me up as I see your health decline. It has to happen to all of us one day, but you are never ready for it. I have always seen you so healthy and energetic that I was not ready to see this sudden change. I definitely am praying for God to heal you and give us this miracle so we can enjoy time with each other for many more years.

Then the song "There is Power in the Blood" played, and I thought of the power of God to heal in every way. Not only can He heal you, He can heal each of us as we struggle to accept whatever He has in store for us. You can see each song gave me something to think about and a piece of encouragement. It was really a wonderful experience listening to each and every one of them.

"Precious Memories" played later, and I could not hold back the tears as I thought about the precious memories of the things God has done and all the precious memories planted deep in my mind over the past forty-five years. The older I get, the more precious the memories become, and the luckier I realize that I am to have had a father and mother like I had. You always gave us the most important things in life: love, shelter, food, prayers, a Christian example, and godly advice. What else could a child ask for?

"Jesus Is the Answer Every Time" is so true, but so many times I have forgotten this and tried to make it through things on my own. Especially when it comes to being a parent. As you know, it is not an easy job, and it does not come with an instruction manual. I wish I had been a more consistent example like you were for me. I know sometimes you also felt like a failure, but I can honestly say to me you have never been a failure. Dad, you are a hero.

"I Come to the Garden Alone" played, and the words were so true in the chorus, He walks with me and talks with me and tells me I am His own. Very true, it is us who forget to listen when He talks. That is me a lot of times, not listening. An area I need improvement in. I find great comfort in knowing that I am one of his own and I am going to try to find more time in my life to go to the garden and listen and talk to God.

"Just a Little Talk with Jesus" played later, and I remember how we used to sing it while driving sometimes and how Gary would echo the low tones. Good ole' times we seem to forget and place little value on. I stopped to thank God for your example again, or who knows where some of your children would be today. Your early seeds took root and are the reason many of us are serving God today and active in a church. Stop and be proud, Dad, you are the inspiration to each of us children far more than you realize. You never need to feel like a failure as a dad. You took your job seriously and did it well! You brought us all up to know Christ—a parent's first and most important task. Well done!

"I'll Fly Away" came on, and I just pictured you flying away to be with God when your time comes and seeing the smile on your face as you rose to the glorious mansion above. Don't take me wrong that I think it will happen anytime soon and that I am not trusting God for the miracle; it was merely a beautiful vision of your excitement to be with the Lord. The testimony that you will leave behind is fabulous. I am sure Jesus will say, "Well done, thou good and faithful servant."

As you can see, each gospel song carried with me a memory. I love the new praise songs, but I also love the old hymns. I do trust God for the miracle of healing and having the opportunity to spend many more years with you, but I also don't want to wait until it is too late to say some of the things I feel. Saying I love you is way to short of a phrase. It says a lot but is merely a portion of how I feel about you and the pride I have in saying you're my dad! You never have to worry about Mom if something happens to you. If Mom was poor, I would see to it she was well taken care of. I will never put her in a home as long as I am able to care for her. You have provided well for her, and I am glad you made mom so happy all these years. You know the meaning of love and dedication.

I see me in you in so many ways. Yes, I'm a blend of both, but, Dad, I have a lot of your traits. Hardworking, goal-oriented, self-sufficient, independent, and sometimes stubborn. Without your example, I do not feel like I would have been successful. You always encouraged me to reach out and achieve what I wanted to accomplish in life, and you taught me the value of believing in myself. Thanks, for this has taken me far. I don't understand why God has blessed me as much as He has, for I am so undeserving.

Well, I guess this is enough to read for now. Hope you have a wonderful day, and I am looking forward to seeing you this weekend.

With love,
Faith

2
Honoring My Father

Over Thanksgiving I headed back to Florida with the intention of bringing my father back to North Carolina with me. This trip did not turn out as I had expected. When I arrived in Florida, my father was weaker than ever, and with every hour he became even weaker. A trip to the doctor was necessary to see if he even had enough energy to make it to North Carolina. The doctor gave my father some tests and discovered that on top of the mesothelioma, he now had developed leukemia. He needed to go straight to the hospital for blood transfusions, or he would die within twenty-four hours. Time was closing in, and I knew his life would come to an end quickly. I would be without my father.

I decided I would stay in Florida with my mother until the end, no matter what was happening with my real estate business back home. I wanted to spend every last minute I could with him and also help my mother, knowing she could not stay in the hospital around the clock with him. After a few days, I took the night shift, allowing Mom to go home and rest. My father did not sleep well, so we were awake most of the nights. The first two weeks he still had his voice, and he was witnessing to everyone with whom he came into contact. He continually made a statement that he was going to win with either of God's decisions for his life. He would say, "If I live, I win, and if I die, I win by going on to heaven with the Lord." He had a rock-solid love for God. While my father was not afraid to die, I knew he did not want to lose precious years with the people he loved. He hated the idea of leaving behind my mother, to whom he had been married for fifty-six years, nor did he want to leave any other family member behind. I could not begin to imagine the thoughts and feelings that must have been running through his heart and mind at this time. While we do not expect perfect health, when sickness and death face us, our spirit senses that this is not the way things were meant to be. I know I questioned God over and over again. I think my father at this point eagerly awaited for the adoption, the redemption of his body as talked about in Romans 8:25. "But if we hope for what we do not see, with perseverance we wait eagerly for it."

He lost his voice completely after they stopped giving him blood transfusions, so communication was in writing for the next few days. Then he became so weak he could not even write. I would write notes to my father, and he would nod if it was what he needed. My father and I still found a way to communicate. It was like I could understand all his groaning and motions and knew how to make him comfortable when no one else did.

We had now switched roles. I wanted to be strong and encourage him like he always encouraged me when I was growing up. I had to care for his needs and lay my own needs aside. I would lay awake all hours of the night to make sure he was okay. I would pray with him like he always prayed with me, and somehow God gave me the strength to hide the tears until he could not see them. I struggled with my emotions as I watched him dying right before my eyes. I could not imagine letting him go when the final moment arrived. All I could do was release him into the hands of the King of kings and Lord of lords.

I had decided since this would be the last Christmas I would have with my father, I would bring him a little Christmas tree thirteen days before Christmas. Each time I came to take my shift, I would bring him ornaments to match and sing "The Twelve Days of Christmas" to him. I spent hours searching for miniature ornaments to match the song and had a lot of fun with it. After the first day, my father would look forward to each group of ornaments I brought and waited in anticipation to see what was next. By Christmas, we had a beautifully decorated little tree, which was the last gift I was able to give my father.

He made it through one last Christmas with his family. Not knowing how long he would hold on, I decided to head home after lunch on Christmas to see my children and grandchildren for one day, knowing I would then head straight back to my father's side. This was a hard decision, but with lots of other family members by his and my mother's side, I headed out with great reluctance. I promised my father before I left that I would be back in two days or less because he wanted me to be with my mother when he went home to be with the Lord. We drove straight through the night and headed to bed. After sleeping about six hours, I received a phone call informing me my father had gone to sleep shortly after midnight, and the doctors said he was slipping into a coma. The doctor felt he would die within twenty-four hours, so immediately I headed straight back to Florida. I could not get a flight since it was during the holiday season, so we jumped back in the car for the twelve-hour ride once again.

Afraid I would not make it before he died, I started praying, "Lord, please keep him alive until I get back. I promised him I would be by my mother's side, and I must see him one more time and tell him I love him once more." Immediately I felt a calm and peace come over me. A still, small voice in my mind was telling me he would be alive when I got there and that he would not let go until I whispered the words of his favorite song in his ear. My dad needed me to communicate with him once more. It was a song written by Carl Boberg, a twenty-six-year-old Swedish minister, titled "How Great Thou Art." After I whispered the words of the song, I knew I would have to turn him loose and let him go.

The drive seemed to go quickly, and we arrived shortly after midnight on December 27. I struggled for a long time just holding his hand, knowing once I sang the song in his ear he would be gone. I could not get the words out for quite some time, so I just sat there stroking his hand. My brother turned to me and said, "Faith, you have to let him go. He has been waiting for you to come back and release him." Then almost everyone left the room. I bent down and whispered in his ear, "Daddy, do you know I am here?" I could feel him try to squeeze my hand, and I started to whisper the words in his ear as tears flowed down my cheeks. I choked on every word but somehow managed to get them out. Now December 27 holds two memories for me: the birth of my first daughter Melissa and the death of my father.

My father considered all the things in the world that God had made. He recognized the power of creation displayed throughout the universe. He had the opportunity to travel all over the world enjoying nature, praising God, and recognizing how great He was. He acknowledged the sacrifice God made when He sent His son to die on the cross, bearing his burdens, bleeding and dying to take away his sin. He knew Christ would return with shouts of acclamation and one day take him home.

I never got the last chorus out, and I could feel his hand grip mine as I told him it was okay to go be with the Heavenly Father. Immediately my father took a deep breath, like a sigh of relief, and his heartbeat dropped rapidly. I know he must have been shouting to the Lord, and joy was filling his heart. I could just picture him bowing at the feet of the Heavenly Father in humble adoration shouting, "My God, how great Thou art!" He loved every word of this song and felt each one from the depths of his heart. In the early morning hours of December 27, 2004, my father went to be with the Lord. Neither my father nor I wanted to let go, but we had to. I was Daddy's little girl until the end, and in my heart I always will be. During the next week, I was in a daze as we buried my father and packed up my mother to move to North Carolina.

3

The Wilderness

All men and women of God will go through difficult seasons. I refer to such a time as being in the wilderness. It is a time in your life when the trail is only wide enough for you and God so God can have personal, intimate time with you. During this time, He attempts to draw you much closer to Him. You begin to see yourself as an individual with the ability to serve God in a greater way. You are away from all comparison and simply one-on-one with God. It is a time when we realize we are not alone in the world or abandoned by God. He is walking beside us ready to help us in our time of need. It is a time where you start to reconsider your priorities and the way you handle things in your life. It is a time where you begin to see yourself the way God sees you.

The wilderness is a wild place where you start out feeling alone, abandoned, and out of control. It is an experience that seems foreign to humans and is difficult to explain, yet you know you are under the care and protection of God throughout the entire journey. You often find you are deep into the wilderness not knowing which direction to turn before you consciously realize what is happening. If we knew ahead of time, we would be tempted to fight and delay the changes God wants to make in our lives. Since it is God's personal time to examine and change your old ways and replace them with a new task just embrace the wilderness time knowing a great spiritual breakthrough is coming. Enjoy the private time building an intimate relationship with the Father. "For our light and momentary troubles are achieving for us an eternal glory that far outweighs them all" (2 Cor. 4:17, NIV). Jesus Himself began His ministry with forty days in the wilderness and ended on a cross, which no doubt was a wilderness experience. I can assure you the eternal glory far outweighed the momentary trouble and suffering Jesus went through.

There are signs indicating we are in a wilderness experience with the Father. Activities in your life will change. What was fun is no longer fun because you begin to hunger and thirst for the Father alone. "Blessed are those who hunger and thirst for righteousness, for they will be filled" (Matt. 5:6, NIV). Character flaws become recognizable and disgusting. We become willing to humble ourselves and allow the Father to change us. Friends often no longer understand you, and some will even desert you. You may observe some persecution as friends see you drawing closer to God and making changes. The Father will give you a new group of friends who will encourage you. They will see Jesus Christ at work in your life and walk with you helping you obtain the goal that is aiming for the prize awaiting you.

Christians are generally surprised by God's power and provision, because their thought process changes when they are experiencing a wilderness encounter. Their spiritual eyes are opened. Their hearts and minds are transformed. They begin to see life in a completely different way as many others have. Many prophets often wandered in the wilderness to be tested. Once they overcame the test, the wilderness became a place of hearing the voice of God. It became a time of spiritual renewal while just basking in the presence of the Father. The Israelites traveled from Egypt into the Promised Land of Canaan after wandering around for forty years. They were surprised many times with the provisions God supplied. The book of Job contains a wonderful description of depending completely on God beyond human understanding and control while encountering time in the wilderness. Job was overloaded with a life full of turmoil. He could not find peace or rest. His friends thought sin brought Job to this stressful time in his life, and he became a mere laughingstock. Job knew God held the life of every creature and the breath of all mankind in His hands. He trusted God until the end when God brought him out of the wilderness. The wilderness time played an important part in the lives of those who were on the journey, and it will do the same for you. The experience often becomes a great spiritual breakthrough as God prepares you for His purposes.

In the book of Revelation you see wilderness as a place of hope and refuge. It is considered a place where the people of God are kept safe. "The woman fled into the wilderness to a place prepared for her by God, where she might be taken care of for 1,260 days" (Rev. 12:6, NIV). "The woman was given the two wings of a great eagle, so that she might fly to the place prepared for her in the wilderness, where she would be taken care of for a time, times and half a time, out of the serpent's reach" (Rev. 12:14, NIV). God prepares a place in the wilderness for you and will sustain you there. It is your divine encounter with the Father so you become more intimate with Him. Don't fight it or reject it. Walk out of the wilderness one day with a great new beginning.

Back in North Carolina ten days later, I started back to work. I had a hard time keeping focused but managed to somehow get houses listed and sold. The death of my father left me feeling lost, wandering in the wilderness. I struggled through various stages of grief. I had to go through the shock, denial, depression, and finally acceptance of the fact that he was gone. I was relying on the Lord for comfort and allowing the healing process to take place. I did not want to roam in the wilderness any longer than necessary. In the wilderness there are too many vicious animals, too much pain from open wounds, and too much grief I needed to turn loose. These things had to be dealt with in order to receive a full restoration and a release from the wilderness. God prepared a place for me in the wilderness. I knew He would sustain me until I found my way out.

Several months passed, and business started to fall into place as usual. Mom was adjusting as best she could. We had settled back into our routine. I found myself praying a lot more than I had before my father's death. In the wilderness I was searching for peace, comfort, and the safety I felt when my father was around. I withdrew somewhat into a shell and had no desire to spend much time with friends. Activities in my life were changing. I would go home early as much as possible to spend time with my mother and do things with her so she would not feel alone. All the time I was feeling alone and lost without my father. Mom was a strong lady, and she seemed to have greater strength than any of her children. She found comfort in knowing her husband was with the Lord and no longer suffering. She always had the right words to say whenever she would see me down. We would cry together at times, and we would laugh together as we shared memories of years past. In the midst of my greatest loss, God was providing the grace I needed to get through this difficult time while drifting in the wilderness.

My mother was moving into my father's role in many ways and getting stronger every day. She was now the one to say, "Let's pray together." She kept up all the traditions Dad had done as if he never left us. I started to see a leader emerge out of my mother—a leader I never noticed before. Mom stepped right up to the plate, being the spiritual leader in the family, not leaving anyone without encouragement and prayer. She always played a big part in ministering to all of her children along with Dad, but seeing the strength in her alone was amazing. It made me greatly appreciate the support she had been to my father. She supported his ministry and stood beside him, encouraging him in every way.

Months passed by so quickly. At the end of the second quarter, during a company sales meeting when the list of individual production was passed out, I realized my business had almost doubled from the previous year. My thoughts went back to the part of my father's prayer where he asked the Lord to bless my business. The blessing had come, and his prayer was being answered. Once I realized the prayer was being answered, I was reminded of the power of a parent's prayer. Thoughts raced through my mind as I remembered the rest of my father's prayer. How was everything my father prayed going to take place? How long would I roam in the wilderness before I could move forward?

My father's prayer would be answered little by little as the Lord prepared my heart. I knew I had lost my joy, but I had no clue how the Lord was going to restore it. I had a hard time accepting the fact that

I had allowed Satan to rob my joy, and I never did anything about it. I went to church almost every Sunday, and I had become quite a good benchwarmer. I would go to church, praise and worship God, hear a message, and then go home and face the world for another week—the same pattern many people fall into when they attend church without realizing they *are* the church. We can easily become complacent because we are not taught how to build an intimate relationship with God. Many churches place too much focus on numbers instead of nurturing. People go to the altar, the pastor baptizes them, but rarely do they have someone to mentor them and help them develop in their Christian life. They are left to figure out where to go from this point, how to deal with their past, and how to build an intimate relationship with their newfound Father. New Christians focus on making changes through their worldly efforts rather than allowing the Holy Spirit to make the changes. They have just accepted Jesus and may not know how the Holy Spirit plays into the equation. Demands by new Christian friends overwhelm many new believers, and their joy and peace begin to deteriorate. I knew I had to find a way to go into the enemy's camp and take back what he stole from me.

It was more than a behavior modification that God was looking for in me. He was looking for a deep and lasting change. My joy and peace had deteriorated, so from this point on I stood on the promise in Jeremiah 31:13, which says, "For I will turn their mourning into joy and will comfort them and give them joy for their sorrow." Although I was experiencing intense sorrow and loss, joy was just around the corner, and it would produce the strength I needed to move forward for God. "Do not be grieved, for the joy of the Lord Is your strength" (Neh. 8:10, NASB).

Knowing something was missing, I set out on a journey, attempting to find my joy in the Lord once again. I wanted to feel whole, complete, and secure in my relationship with Jesus. I knew I needed to be firmly grounded. I was coming to Jesus, asking for His guidance to find peace and joy. I was casting all my burdens on Him, and I knew He cared for me. "Humble yourselves under the mighty hand of God, that He may exalt you at the proper time, casting all your anxiety on Him, because He cares for you" (1 Pet. 5:6–7, NASB). Humbly placing my burden in the hands of God, I knew in His timing I would be set free. My desire was to please Him—and that would please my dad as well. Even though he was gone, Daddy's little girl always tried to please him.

Holidays soon approached as the year was coming to an end. Dreading the first Thanksgiving and Christmas seasons without my father, all I could think about was the last month of his life spent through this same time frame just one year earlier. Thanksgiving and Christmas came and went, but the prior year's memories hung with everyone in the family. The year had come to an end, and I was looking forward to 2006. I made a New Year's resolution to diligently seek God for restoration of the joy in Him I had lost so I could find my way out of the wilderness. I planned to look under every tree, in every hole, at the bottom of the river, and not leave any rock unturned until I could find peace and joy.

Ephesians 2:14 says, "For He Himself is our peace." Peace and joy are gifts you receive from Jesus if you are grafted into the vine. God wants to be close to us. A branch and a vine are connected, and when you snip the branch from the vine, the branch will die. It is no longer growing or able to produce fruit. It works the same way in our relationship with God. We have to stay connected and allow Him to nourish us.

I was grafted into the vine, and nothing could separate me from Him unless I allowed it. Being a child of God was merely a start. He wants a relationship with his children as a friend; He wants to know you will not turn your back on Him and betray Him. He may need to modify your behavior, or He may need a deeper change from you. Jesus came to preach peace and joy, and the only person who can keep you from having these gifts is you. As John 14:26 says, when you accept Jesus, He becomes your comforter. You receive the helper—the Holy Spirit whom the Father sent to teach you all things. I turned to Him for help just like I did my father up until his death. I no longer could call my father and let him comfort me, but I could call on Jesus for comfort and on the Holy Spirit for help. The Holy Spirit is essential for all believers for He is the One Jesus called to be our helper. The Holy Spirit was right there trying to help me, and I had merely tuned Him out.

I started tuning in to the voice of the Holy Spirit, and I began to hear. I had taken time to settle down and be still so I could listen. When Jesus and His disciples came to the village where Martha opened up her house, her sister Mary sat at the feet of Jesus listening to everything He had to say. Martha was distracted by all the preparations, and she became very frustrated with Mary for sitting down and not offering a helping hand. She had the audacity to go to Jesus and ask Him to tell Mary to help her. Martha did not even see the importance of sitting still with her mouth shut just listening to Jesus and hearing what He had to say (Luke 10:38–42, paraphrased). I had reached a place and time in my life where sitting still and listening became my priority. There may be more than one thing I needed in life, but I was after what was most important.

On the second Sunday of 2006, while driving to a church the family had been attending for nearly twelve years, we passed New Life Church. Something was tugging at my heart to visit the church as we drove by. After I mentioned it to the family, we decided to turn around and visit. The church had a warm, friendly feeling, and it felt like home. I did not feel like a visitor but felt like part of the family. It felt like this was the church I had been attending for a long time, and it was where we belonged. Everyone was very friendly, many introduced themselves, and our family felt welcome. Something about New Life Church seemed to draw me in, and as a family we decided to continue going to New Life for a while and see if God wanted us there.

After attending for six weeks, I started to feel like God had planted me there for a reason. I was learning, and every message challenged me to make changes in my life. It was more than listening to a sermon; it was listening to a teacher share a lesson. I wondered if this was how the crowds felt when Jesus spoke. People must have been able to shut out the world and focus on the one teaching, for there was so much to learn. My desires were changing as I sought to know God like He knows me. I wanted a personal, intimate relationship with God like I had with my father. I wanted a deeper relationship than I had ever had in the past—a bond and closeness so great I would miss Him when I took Him out of the picture, just like I had been missing my father since he had passed away. I knew I had to seek God for the answers and listen. What if I missed His voice? Could I really communicate with Him like I communicated with my father? Could we have conversations and relate to one another? You better believe you can. God spoke to people throughout the Bible. There are hundreds of inspiring stories where God talks to His people. So why would He stop speaking to us today? He won't; we have just stopped listening. How could you have an intimate relationship with someone who never communicates with you? You can't.

Seeking the Father, I started to pray, "Lord Jesus, help me to have an intimate relationship with You. Change me and show me the path You have chosen for my life, the path that will lead me out of the wilderness and into the valley of peace toward my destiny for You." I was learning to feel the love of the Heavenly Father and to allow Him to replace the emptiness I felt from the loss of my father. I knew if I was willing, the Holy Spirit would start guiding and directing me every step of the way. I prayed daily for the Holy Spirit to show me what I needed to do to find real joy and peace like I once had. I prayed for wisdom and understanding as I continued to seek the Heavenly Father for correction and direction for my life.

God was preparing me for a life-changing journey as He was increasing my measure of faith and restoring our Father-daughter relationship. I, like many others, needed a deep cleansing. I had to dig deeply and remove everything causing separation between God and me. Isaiah 59:2 says, "But your iniquities have made a separation between you and your God, and your sins have hidden His face from you so that He does not hear." How could God hear me if I had any sin hiding His face from me? If you are not hearing God, you may need to examine yourself. As it says in Psalm 66:18, "If I regard wickedness in my heart, the Lord will not hear." A full cleansing had to be completed so God could hear me and answer my prayers. With a total cleansing, I could have a victorious relationship with God—and I was going after it. The more you are willing to empty yourself, the more space you have to open for the Holy Spirit to fill.

Months went by, and every Sunday during the message the Holy Spirit was speaking to me. It felt like the pastor knew everything I needed to hear and was speaking directly to me. Sometimes the message hit so hard I felt like a twenty-pound weight was dropped into my lap and I could not move. I would go home and ponder the message for the entire week and fall on my face before God. I had so much to learn as I realized I barely knew God. I had only scratched the surface of knowing the Father who had given everything, including His only begotten Son, for me.

Why had I put so much effort into pleasing my father and so little into pleasing my Heavenly Father? Was it because I could physically see the delight in my father's eyes and not picture the delight in God's eyes? He has to be even more delighted when He knows we try to please Him. Why was it so difficult to put distance between my father-daughter relationship but not as painful to put distance between the Father-daughter relationship? I loved my father so much it was hard to let him go, and yet I often let go of my Heavenly Father. How could I have diligently worked at doing things to perfection for my father and put so little effort into the things the Heavenly Father asked me to do? I had taken time to communicate with my father and listen to his words of encouragement, but my communication with the Heavenly Father was weak. I know I could have found words of encouragement and affirmation many times had I only looked and listened for them. I had many changes to make, and my Father had patience as He brought things to my attention one by one. God worked on me—little by little, piece by piece—never giving me more than I could bear. He brought to light people I needed to forgive, things I needed to repent of, people I needed to love unconditionally, things I needed to turn loose, thought patterns I needed to change, attitudes I needed to adjust, and many other things I had to deal with in my life.

A short time later I started feeling convicted over my real estate business. I prayed about my business and prayed for sellers and buyers, but I still ran business my way. I trusted God to provide and direct my business, but I realized I had not truly given my business to Him. I had not committed it to His glory. I thought I had, but now God was showing me differently. God wanted me to commit my business to Him fully—in every way, with no strings attached—totally and unconditionally. God wanted me to allow Him to run it and use it as a ministry for His service, and He was directing me to be a servant in a new way. My view of life was changing, and I no longer could do things the way I had before. I was a wet ball of clay in the center of the potter's hand, and He was busily starting to form me into His intended image.

Spiritual transformation was taking place at such a rapid pace I found myself questioning if it was all God or if my mind was interfering. I was finally meeting with the One who was always there for me. As I was growing spiritually, I wanted to be sure I was hearing from God, and I did not allow myself to interfere and alter His intent in any way. I eagerly looked forward to attending the upcoming fall revival meetings and learning even more about the Lord. My soul was thirsty for more knowledge of the Heavenly Father, so I diligently kept looking. With this burning desire in my heart, I knew I was still not walking in the full joy of the Lord. I repented each time the Holy Spirit convicted me of something and did not dismiss it until I found freedom.

A piece of the puzzle was still missing, and I was going to find it. Once again I pondered the question "What must I do to get my full joy back?" Without joy, I could not be open to His divine will for my life. How could I possibly do the will of the Father without a joyous heart? I wanted the joy I felt as I pleased my earthly father, and I knew my Heavenly Father wanted and deserved even greater. Pleasing the Father is an area you must continually work at if you are seeking an intimate relationship with Him. We cannot keep a few of the commands in the Bible and leave others out. God wants us to take every command seriously and strive toward holiness.

In Exodus 19, Moses went up to God and called to Him from the mountain. In the following verses the people were given the option of obeying and keeping the Lord's covenant and moving to a new level of intimacy with the Heavenly Father. "You yourselves have seen what I did to the Egyptians, and how I bore you on eagles wings, and brought you to Myself. Now then, if you will indeed obey My voice and keep My covenant, then you shall be My own possession among all the peoples, for all the earth is Mine and you shall be to Me a kingdom of priests and a holy nation" (Exod. 19:4–6, NASB).

As children of the Father, we have been pulled out of our sin and out of the world, yet we still live like most of the people in the world. We have become satisfied with so many traditions living in the comfort of the four walls of the church. We listen to the wisdom of leaders and teachers, become program-driven, go to meeting after meeting, serve on committees, and have overlooked the idea that God is trying to make us His people. He is still taking people from every class and culture and planting His character in them. He is continually building a Bride, and He is coming back one day to take the Bride home.

With an upcoming week of revival, I looked forward to more time in the presence of the Lord. When you go before the Lord with expectations of finding Him, He shows up. I was reaching out for all I could grasp and ready to receive everything He had to give me. The first evening was refreshing as the message reinforced many of the encounters I was experiencing with the Holy Spirit during the past few months. Revival was being birthed in me because I was seeking Him. It was more than just a meeting with a guest speaker; it was like being on a date, and I left feeling one step closer to my Father. I went home, headed to bed, and quickly fell asleep. Within a few hours I was suddenly awakened from a dream. I was perplexed and thought the dream must have been meant for someone else. I dreamed I was standing before the congregation, pouring out the reasons I was afraid to be all God wanted me to be and repenting so I could be restored to a joyous relationship with Him. The last part sounded great, but the first part would be too humiliating. I did not remember dreaming the reasons for my fear but knew I had some pretty serious issues causing me to be afraid. It felt so real once I woke up. I was even more afraid and could not go back to sleep. It was beyond my imagination to think I was afraid to be all God wanted me to be. I merely wasn't ever asked to do much, nor was I knowledgeable enough. Thinking that surely God would not ask me to do this in public, I buried my head in my pillow and cried out, "Lord, what is this all about?" I did not want to believe or accept that I was afraid of being all God wanted me to be. I asked, "Lord, please show me why I am afraid."

The rest of the night, God started revealing to me all the reasons I was afraid of Him. I started remembering circumstances in my life contributing to this fear I never thought about—Flashes of times when I was tempted to sin and I gave in to the schemes of the enemy, failure in my first marriage while all the time I loved and tried to serve the Lord, times people laughed at me, times I felt rejected, times I merely did not feel good enough, and many more circumstances that had built up a wall of fear. The wall had become high and thick. Humbled, broken, and with tear-filled eyes, I realized I was afraid to be all God wanted me to be. I was afraid my husband would walk out on me, afraid of what people would think of me, afraid that God may ask me to do something for Him I wasn't ready or equipped to do, afraid I may fail at serving Him the way He wanted me to, and afraid of facing the unknown. I realized it was a lifelong journey to commit to God's divine will—and it was scary. Ashamed, I just lay there crying. How could I be afraid of the Father in this way? How could I fear being directed by the unconditionally loving Father? No wonder I was confined to the wilderness. Before I could transition out of the wilderness, I had to remove my fears. I should only be afraid of not doing the will of the Father.

While I lay there feeling ashamed, I felt the loving arms of someone unseen holding on to me tightly. I felt a warm feeling I had never felt before as I pondered the thoughts of being afraid to be all God wanted me to be. Why was I afraid to confess Him before others? Jesus was not afraid to stand up to the Heavenly Father on my behalf. No matter what mistakes I made, Jesus was ready to plead my case before the Heavenly Father. What was wrong with me that I was afraid of the unknown with the One who loved me the most? You should never be afraid of your best friend. I asked God to forgive me once again and show me how to find victory over this fear, knowing it had to go. I had to have more confidence in the Heavenly Father than I did in my dad, and I always felt safe with him.

The next day, I could not stay focused on work at all. I got in my car and drove around for hours just trying to sort out the dream and the thoughts racing through my mind. As I drove around, the Holy Spirit started speaking to me and showing me how I could find freedom. I must be willing to confess publicly and lay down my fear. I had to do as I dreamed—share it and lay it down before others so I could walk in victory. I had to publicly apologize to my husband and children for not being all God wanted me to be. If I had been in the divine plan of God, I would have been a better wife and mother. Realizing this was true only made me feel sicker than I already felt. How could I possibly confess and apologize in front of a church full of strangers? If I had to do this publicly, how on earth would I get through it? Getting through this could only happen if I set aside all pride and allowed the Holy Spirit to direct me and strengthen me at the right time. This would be minor humiliation compared to what Jesus went through for you and me. Jesus was humiliated in public, mocked, laughed at, spit upon, beaten, whipped, pierced with a crown of thorns, and forced to drag His own cross, on which He was crucified. What reason did I have to fear just making a simple public confession?

Two days later, the thought of public confession was still on my mind. Giving in, I knew this was not going to go away until I dealt with my fear the way God wanted it dealt with. I accepted that things do not always unfold the way I would like them to. I had to make the decision now whether I would go forward in my walk with Christ, if I was going to stand still, or—worse yet— if I was going to go backward. God was after me and calling me to a higher level of commitment and a deeper relationship with Him, and this was just one more step I had to take.

The next morning, I woke up feeling it was the day to take care of laying down my fear. In my mind, I thought it was too soon—that I needed more time to muster up the courage—but God knew there was no reason to put this off. I knew it would not get any easier, and I just needed to get it behind me. I left work early in the afternoon to go home, feeling tired and scared. This thought had haunted me for three days and nights, and I desperately needed sleep. I fell on my knees, praying and asking God for strength stronger than I had ever felt before and the courage to be obedient to Him. I had the feeling that God wanted to use me as an example for others to see their need to lay down all of their own fears. If it would help one other person, it would be worth it all—but why not let someone else be used as an example? I knew I could lay down my fear in private a whole lot more easily, but God knew differently. He knew if I did it privately, it would be much easier to pick the fear back up, and He knew it would be an encouragement to others who were dealing with the same issue. In order to obtain intimacy with God, you have to experience a certain level of brokenness.

With adrenaline racing through my body, I rushed out the door early for the evening revival meeting to spend time in the prayer room. I knew the intercessors met early each evening to pray for the service, and I needed their prayer. I shared with the intercessors in the room that God was showing me something in my life and that He wanted me to share it with the church tonight. I asked for prayer, and immediately the group encircled me and started to pray over me. I left the room and headed toward the sanctuary with my red, swollen eyes, feeling a little calmer and encouraged, trusting God would help me get through it. I hoped the speaker had a short message and I could get it over with quickly.

The evening service started, and I almost fell off the bench when the guest speaker stood up to speak and shared the title of his message. He said he wanted to speak to us this evening about fear factors and how they had to be removed in order to be all God wanted us to be. I knew my confession was definitely part of God's timing. He had brought it to the surface in my life so today I could walk in victory and lay down my fear at the foot of the cross. Many people have fear factors in their lives, but few recognize them and are willing to turn them over to God. I was ready and willing to turn it loose.

As the message came to an end, I could feel butterflies fluttering in my stomach, and I knew the time was close. The invitation was given for us to search our lives and confess any fear factors we may have—but there was no need for me to search; mine were already found. The pastor asked if there was anyone who was willing to share their fears and invited them to come forward. Heading toward the front of the church, I knew it was time to lay down the fears keeping me from moving forward in my relationship with my Father. As I spoke, God provided comfort, and the words came out far more easily than I expected. I could feel freedom coming over me as I shared how my past had caused me to build up fear—a fear I had not even realized, a fear that if I was all Christ wanted me to be I would be rejected and left alone. Laying down all my fear, I committed my life to be all God wanted me to be—no matter what the cost, no matter who liked or disliked me, and no matter who laughed at me. I publicly apologized to my husband for not being the wife I could have been in the first fourteen years of our marriage if I had walked in God's divine will. I also apologized to my two daughters for not being the mother I could have been if I had been all God wanted me to be. Being only part of what God wants us to be does not allow us to be the best we can. God is such a loving Father, and we need to be all He wants us to be and make Him proud of us. Wow! What instant freedom! The weight of a heavy brick was removed, and I was ready for the change. I wanted my excitement and joy back, and I was ready to continue to work on the Father-daughter relationship.

I met a friend also dealing with fears of her own. She was raised in a family that struggled financially, and she lived with the fear of losing everything she had and being poor once again. Satan used this as a way to keep her distracted from all God wanted to do in her life. She spent hours pondering ways to keep from becoming poor and going backward financially. This fear bound her so tightly that eventually it happened. Her husband lost his business, and they lost their personal home as well. She went into the wilderness, wondering where God was, when she realized that she was one of the richest women alive. She had her husband, her two children, food, and clothing. God provided a new job for her husband, but greater yet, she knew she had Jesus and that she was a child of God. She found an abundance of wealth just by resting in the arms of the Heavenly Father and trusting Him to restore her and bring her out of the wilderness.

Far too many people live in a world of fear, not realizing that fear can destroy them. Many earthly circumstances and situations cause fear, and you can be so afraid of things happening that you end up getting what you expect. You need to rest in the arms of God and realize you have nothing to fear if you are one of His children. God never gives you more than you can handle, and He never puts you in situations He does not equip you for. He always gives us a way out if we are depending on Him. He does not want you to be afraid of where He may lead you and what He may ask you to do. "I had sought the Lord and He answered me; He delivered me from all my fears" (Ps. 34:4, NASB). I was in a divine encounter with the Father, and I would only grow closer to Him.

Study Questions

Do you remember a time when you felt like you were in the wilderness just wandering around trying to find a new direction? Did you try to draw closer to God, or did you find yourself pulling away? If you did pursue Him even harder, how did you go about it? What changes came about in your life through the experience?

Do you spend time praying for others? Do you share your needs with others to pray for you?

Do you know how to build an intimate relationship with the Heavenly Father? Do you know where to begin and what steps you need to take to keep it growing?

Do you have sin you have not sought forgiveness for causing separation between you and the Father?

Do you spend more time pleasing people instead of God?

The loss of a loved one is very hard on us when we have to deal with the separation. Do you find it hard when you put separation between you and God?

What is keeping you from having full joy in Jesus Christ?

Do you go to church with expectations of meeting with the King?

Do you fear allowing God to have full control over your life?

What fears are you holding on to which need to be laid down at the feet of Jesus?

4

Change Begins

"Those who look to Him are radiant; their faces are never covered with shame" (Ps. 34:5, NIV). I was no longer living in fear. There was no shame on my face, and I was radiant. The next part of my father's prayer was answered. Parents should never underestimate the power of the prayers they pray to the Heavenly Father for their children, nor should they ever stop praying for them. I am sure my father experienced many prayers being answered regarding his children, and many of them are still being answered today. My joy was back, and the restoration process continued. I eagerly sought after God in a new and deeper way. My prayer life continued growing, and I was learning to listen for the voice of God. I had to slow down and take time to listen and let things happen at His pace. Once I slowed down, not only did I find time; I gained the desire to speak with God and not just pray out of habit. Seriously reading the Bible, I began to see the Father in a new way. I was learning to know more of His attributes and personality and learning how to better communicate with Him. I thought back to when I was a teenager and my father and I had to focus sometimes when we tried to communicate with each other. We had to learn how to blend our personalities and understand from where the other was coming. We had to take time to patiently listen to each other and communicate back and forth until we understood each other. Although the Heavenly Father understands everything about us, we must get off the one-way street and try to understand everything we possibly can about Him.

Studying the characteristics of Jesus, I was getting a clearer picture of what the Father looked like. You can also have the characteristics of Jesus by allowing the Holy Spirit to direct you and transform your mind. Allowing the Holy Spirit to take over my thoughts, my desires in life were changing rapidly. Knowing God has a specific plan and purpose, I continued seeking His will for my life—unlike when I still contributed to the choice. Instead, I was willing to do His divine will, knowing the outcome would glorify Him. I continued to empty myself and replace the emptiness by allowing the Holy Spirit to occupy the space.

"Then I heard the voice of the Lord, saying, "Whom shall I send, and who will go for Us?" Then I said, "Here am I. Send me!" (Isa. 6:8, NIV). When you get to the point you are willing to do the divine will of the Heavenly Father, He will show up and lead you in a new direction. He is always looking for willing people He can send to build the kingdom. I had come to a place in my life where God met me in the path and said, "I will pick you up and turn you in a different direction. I have a new path, and I want to send you on a journey down it." Once you are standing in the intersection, you cannot be afraid. You simply must trust that your Father knows what He is doing with your life and trust He will guide and direct you every step of the way. Acknowledge that the Father knows best. "I said, 'you are my servant; I have chosen you and have not rejected you. So do not fear, for I am with you; do not be dismayed, for I am your God. I will strengthen you and help you; I will uphold you with my righteous right hand'" (Isa. 41:9–10, NIV). Are you His servant? If so, you have nothing to fear—He will strengthen you every step of the way.

"In all your ways acknowledge Him and He will direct your path" (Prov. 3:6, KJV). I was allowing the Father to direct my path, and all He requested from me was to follow His directions. I was drawn to the Father for His guidance. I was surrendering to Him so I could walk away with a deeper holiness. Do you acknowledge Him and allow Him to direct your path? Do you want a deeper holiness with the Father? He is much more reliable than the highest-priced global positioning system you can purchase. Why not turn on your GPS and listen to the voice that will tell you how to reach your destination? You place more confidence in the voice of your GPS than you do in hearing the voice of God for directions. God has a global position for each and every one of His children. You must find your position and be willing to follow His directions to get to your destination. It takes more effort to tune into His voice, and the directions may lead you somewhere you are not willing to go—but you need to go there anyway.

In the past, I rebelled against God's directions just like I had my father's at times. I tried to mainly work for God within the four walls of church building, keeping God contained in a box. Within the walls of the church, I had taught Sunday school, sang in the choir, directed a children's choir, and helped in the nursery. I tried to work wherever there was a need and was not concerned about where I was gifted or how I was to use my spiritual gifts. In fact, I am not even sure I knew what my spiritual gifts were—just like many others don't know.

Searching to find what my gifts were and how and where I was to use them, I took two different spiritual gifts tests and started praying for clarity and confirmation. If I was part of the body of Christ, then I had to be the part He had assigned for me. 1 Corinthians 12:14–19 says, "For the body is not one member, but many. If the foot says, 'because I am not a hand, I am not a part of the body,' it is not for this reason any the less a part of the body. And if the ear says, 'because I am not an eye, I am not a part of the body,' it is not for this reason any less a part of the body. If the whole body were an eye, where would the hearing be? If the whole were hearing, where would the sense of smell be? But now God has placed the members, each one of them, in the body just as He desired. If they were all one member, where would the body be?"

The world tells us we are nobody, but to God, we are a very significant part of building the Kingdom. We think we need to be perfected in every way before we can be useful, so we sit for years and do nothing. All God is asking is that everyone we meet sees Christ in us. He will give us the words to speak life into them and make a difference. God did not send His Son to shed His blood and die on the cross so we could be brought into the kingdom and merely take up space. He wants us to realize that every encounter we have every day of our lives is important and that every person is important. Jesus shed His blood for everyone, not just the people saved. Our ministry needs to be wherever we are at every moment of our lives. Yet my ministry was contained in a box.

While I tried to contain my ministry within the walls of the church, God was trying to place my ministry in the secular world. I meet many lost people through my real estate business, and I had numerous opportunities to share Christ with people. I also meet many who believe in Jesus and need encouragement, need to hear truth, need spiritual or physical healing, need deliverance from the past, need to be freed from demons, need to feel unconditional love, need financial help, and numerous other needs. I had been passing up opportunity after opportunity, and the Father was disappointed with my neglect to share Him with others. I needed to be consciously aware of the opportunities to share Christ without hesitation when the door was open. I had to be ready to jump in with words and prayers, ministering to others and bringing glory to God. I had to share my Father and take Him out of the box. I remember playing with my jack-in-the-box as a child. I would wind up the crank over and over again until it could not be wound up any tighter. Jack would pop open the lid and jump out at me. I would jump every time even though I knew it was going to happen. This is how we need to be with the Heavenly Father. We need to be so wound up about Him that the crank is tight and He is popping out in everything we do and everywhere we go. He should show up and surprise everyone we meet with something new. This would involve thinking like Jesus thought, discerning the needs of others, and being willing to minister to them. I had to allow myself to be directed by the power and presence of Holy Spirit—to walk like a disciple at all times. I needed to learn to hear His voice clearly and be willing to obey whatever the Father would ask.

I worked hard at obeying my father, listening to his voice, and following his directions because I wanted to please him and be Daddy's little girl. I had not given the Heavenly Father this same respect. I had never worked as hard to please God as I had my father. Diligently serving God involves a full sacrifice of self and a total commitment to Him—no matter what the cost. I had to be willing without any reservation, and so do you. You cannot alter God's plans in any way.

God desired to use my business to advance the Kingdom of God in more ways than one. Daily I asked God, "Continue stripping my heart of self; fill it more and more with You." I prayed for wisdom and understanding as I read the Bible to a greater level than I ever had in the past. I stood on the promise in James 1:5–6: "If any of you lacks wisdom, he should ask God, who gives generously to all without finding fault, and it will be given to him. But when he asks, he must believe and not doubt." You and I are part of the "all," and He will give us wisdom generously. I prayed for an understanding of His divine plan for my life regarding His Kingdom so I could move into my position. I had turned on my internal GPS (God's Positioning System) to search for His plans for my life that I had overlooked. I was focused on listening to every turn and following His directions to get to my destination.

Now that I was tuned into the voice of God, He was instructing me, and He started visiting me through dreams and visions. The eyes of this blind woman had been opened, and the ears of this deaf lady could now hear. With eyes open, I had a vision one day that brought me to my knees. As a real estate broker, I go through many doors. Before me I saw rows and rows of doors. If I knocked or rang the doorbell, the door was opened for me, and I would enter. I saw myself walk through these doors day after day, taking myself inside the homes. I had Jesus inside me, and I kept Him there. I never ushered Him in the door with me. I never invited Him to speak at these appointments. I never introduced Him as my friend. I rarely shared Him with others. It was all about business and keeping it on the professional level. Just like the old saying "You don't mix business and politics," many believe you don't mix business and religion. Before my face flashed hundreds and hundreds of doors with Jesus standing outside them—and I just shut them in His face as I went inside. In the vision, I could feel Him pounding in my heart like the pounding on a door, wanting to come out and stand beside me. Feeling guilty, I cried out to God for forgiveness. I hurt because I knew I hurt my Father, and He was the best friend I ever had or could have. Then I was given a new picture. The new vision had hundreds and hundreds of doors being opened again. I was given a second chance, and this time we walked into the homes side by side. With robust excitement, I took Jesus by the hand and ushered Him through the door with me. I let Him speak, and I introduced Him as my friend. He was sitting at the table with me, instructing and teaching. I was excited about sharing Him, and I no longer cared only about being professional regarding real estate. I also sought to be professional in my knowledge of Him so I could share with accuracy. Jesus went right in the door with me, and He was part of the conversation. He was the highlight of the appointment. Now I was building memories to cherish forever with my Heavenly Father.

When you take Jesus with you through the open doors, you will be amazed at what can happen. On one occasion, I went to list a house and was given only two weeks in which to sell it or it would be listed with another real estate firm. I thought there was no way possible to accomplish this, but I was willing to give it my best effort. While in the home, taking photos for advertising, the Holy Spirit started speaking to me and telling me to commit the house to God, along with the commission I would earn, and it would be sold. I was directed to march around the perimeter of the property and give it to the Lord.

I had a much better picture of how Joshua must have felt when God directed him to take the city of Jericho. He was directed to take seven priests carrying seven trumpets, take the Ark of the Covenant along with the armed men, and march around the city of Jericho once every day for six days. Then on the seventh day, they were to march around the city seven times. On the seventh time around, the priests were to blow the trumpets with a loud blast, and all the people were instructed to shout. Joshua had everyone do exactly as God directed. God showed up, the walls tumbled down, and the people were able to seize the city. They collected the gold, silver, bronze, and iron, which were sacred to the Lord and placed it all in the treasury as God had instructed.

So I was marching around the property, talking out loud to God, dedicating it for His glory, and thanking God in advance for the sale of the house. I marched from corner to corner, following the Father's instructions and trusting Him to be faithful in His promise. After getting in my car to leave, I was prompted to mark ten days out on my calendar as the day of the sale. For the next ten days, I thanked God every day for bringing a buyer. I shared this encounter with a few friends, and on the tenth day, someone called me in the morning to see if the house was sold. I stated that the day had just started, and it would be sold by evening. All day I thanked God for selling the home, and at 5:00 p.m., I received an offer. You better believe I was shouting and blowing my trumpet for the Lord because we had a signed and accepted cash contract by 8:00 p.m. All the walls Satan put up came tumbling down, and God received all the glory.

The next door that was open created multiple opportunities for the Heavenly Father to be glorified. Receiving a call from a pastor visiting his mother in North Carolina, I was asked to come and look at her property, which they wanted to sell. He deeply desired to sell her home and move her to Pennsylvania to live with him and his wife because her health was declining. Visiting his mother's home, I knew I was facing a challenge. She lived in a beautiful, double-wide mobile home on a private lot. In the current market numerous similar properties were being foreclosed and sold for one half of what was needed out of her home site. Sitting at the dining room table, the four of us started talking about the Lord. I shared with them the challenge we were facing, and we prayed together before I left. We placed the home in the hands of the Lord, trusting Him to provide a buyer at the price they needed.

The next day we put up a sign—and I received a call the same evening. I scheduled a time to take them to preview the home the following morning. After working with them and their lender for a few days, they put a contract on the property, and it would go to closing in four weeks.

During the loan process period, many new doors were opened. This pastor invited me to his church in Pennsylvania to share with his congregation the blessings of giving your business to the Lord. I was also asked to do a thirty-minute interview on a Christian television broadcast when I visited in Pennsylvania.

The week prior to closing on the property, his elderly mother injured her back and wound up in the hospital. Doctors informed the family that she would never fully recover or be able to live on her own again. I thanked and praised the Lord over and over again for his provision in selling the home for He already knew this was going to happen. He had worked out all the details, leaving nothing undone. Her son arrived in Hickory, overwhelmed by the many decisions to be made and the workload awaiting. He didn't know whether his mother would be able to travel or if she would end up in a nursing home and never get to make the move and be close to him. He had so much packing to do in order to be out of the home in just a few days.

The need was expressed to various members of the body of Christ, and an abundance of love flowed out as brothers and sisters—most unknown to this family—united and joined together to take the burden off this pastor. Arrangements were made to pack, load the truck, drive the truck to Pennsylvania along with an additional vehicle, provide a place for him to stay, and make arrangements to get his mother transported by plane to a senior citizens' facility in Pennsylvania for rehab. It was a time when I witnessed a unified body of believers pulling together from various congregations to fulfill the need in the family of God. The questions and instructions given in James 2:14–17 applied to this situation. What good is it if a man claims to have faith but has no deeds? Can faith alone save him? James goes on to say that if a brother or sister is in need, will we tell them to go and wish them well and do nothing about their physical needs? What good would this be? Faith by itself not accompanied by actions is dead. The body of Christ pulled together in this case—these believers had actions, and they were alive and willing to reach out in love, helping their brother and sister in need.

On another occasion, when called to list a home, I arrived and quickly realized I was on a greater mission. It was more than listing and selling a house. As the homeowners walked around showing me their property, I kept getting the impression that someone needed healing. I wasn't sure if it was a physical or spiritual healing (or maybe both). When we got back to the kitchen and the three of us stood around their bar, I asked them why they were selling their home. Financial pressures had put a strain on them, and the gentleman started telling me about a declining health condition. He had open wounds in his stomach from a staph infection, which continued to get bigger and bigger, and he had more wounds opening up. As he talked, I knew God wanted his heart. God wanted this man to trust in Him and be healed. When he finished speaking, I asked him if he believed in God. Choked up, he replied that he did. I asked if I could pray with him and told him the Lord wanted to heal him and mend his heart. He was willing, so the three of us stopped and prayed at once. The power and presence of the Holy Spirit permeated the room. With tears flowing down his cheeks, the man started pouring out his lack of faith in God, his belief, and his lack of serving and commitment. We talked for over an hour as his heart was drawn to reconcile, repent, and commit to serving God. His wife, broken as well, joined in the conversation, and the true reason for the appointment was fulfilled. God is in the heart-healing business.

Several weeks later, I had the opportunity to speak with them once again and hear about all the things God was doing in their lives. He was telling everyone about his encounter and sharing Jesus with everyone he came in contact with. He shared with me that the Lord had called him to preach when he was younger, and he did not do it. Although he may never pastor a church, he was now fulfilling the calling and preaching Christ all over his hometown. He took time to share Christ everywhere he went. He realized how significant his part in building the kingdom was, which he had overlooked for years. He was bubbling over with joy, feeling at peace with God, and trusting God for a complete physical healing. The door had been open; I walked through it. Spiritual healing had taken place, and physical healing would come.

Six months later this same gentleman came by my office and wanted to talk to me. I took him in the conference room, and he said he came to tell me the Lord had healed him physically as well. He pulled up his shirt and showed me the once open pit in his stomach. It was sealed up completely. As tears flooded down his cheeks, he just kept praising God for healing him and giving him the opportunity to preach one more time. I cried right with him and thanked the Lord as well. Not only was he telling people what the Lord had done for him, I was sharing it with everyone I came in contact with for months.

These are just a few of the many encounters I experienced taking Jesus through the doors with me. With anticipation and excitement, I look forward to every open door, not knowing what I will find on the other side. The Holy Spirit will be there to guide and direct any situation presenting itself. I continued on my journey, seeking the face of God, allowing the Master Himself to lead and teach me. He was the light leading me through the dark trails in the wilderness. Every time I started to stumble, He would shine the light even brighter. If I started to make a wrong turn, He provided proper directions.

Study Questions

Are you a true servant of God? What changes would you have to make if Jesus became you? Would the change go unnoticed, or would it surprise others?

Does God direct the path of your life? Do you acknowledge Him, His will, and His ways and give Him full control?

Do you know what your gifts, abilities, and talents are to do your work for the Kingdom of God? Are you fulfilling your part in the body of Christ?

How do you see yourself on a daily basis? Do other people see Jesus in you?

Do you claim to have faith yet do not have good deeds to back up your faith? If faith without actions is dead, are you dead or alive?

Do you know how to walk through open doors and share Jesus Christ with others?

How much effort do you put into thinking and acting like Jesus?

Are you comfortable praying with strangers and friends?

5

A New Direction

I continued my journey through the wilderness, moving forward down the straight and narrow path. By now I had come to realize being in the wilderness is not all bad. I remembered how Jesus Himself would often slip away into the wilderness to pray and spend time getting close to His Father (Luke 5:16, paraphrased). If being in the wilderness is how I would get to know God and build our Father-daughter relationship, it was worth the time spent.

Another year had gone by since I buried my earthly father, and a new Father was taking over—the Father who is the same yesterday, today, tomorrow, and forever. The One who will never leave you nor forsake you. The One who will guide you throughout life if you give Him the opportunity. I was allowing God to guide me into the plans He had for my life and learning to talk to Him more about the things that concerned me. God has a plan for everyone, and this was just the beginning of His future plans for me now that I had become a follower and not just a believer. I was learning to hear His voice more clearly and recognize when He was speaking to me. As children of God, it is easy to pass thoughts and impressions off as sheer insight—or better still, women can pass it off as female intuition. Don't ignore the still, small voice in your head or impressions that are laid upon your heart. Start noticing the little things and you will receive even greater revelation.

I could hear the Heavenly Father telling me over and over again how much He loved me—just like my dad told me. His love felt stronger, more comforting and intense, and easier to grasp; it was a much deeper feeling of love than I had ever felt before. I was so thankful that I was discovering the warmth of His love. I was hungry, thirsty, and I knew there had to be more than what I possessed. The Father was calling me to chase after Him with all my heart. I had been trying to hide from Him long enough. He was right there with wide-open arms waiting to receive me. I was reading the Bible every chance I had, searching for the treasures buried within the pages. I wanted to restore my relationship with the Heavenly Father and live a more abundantly filled life. I longed to be delivered from the past and restored to an intimate relationship with Him. I wanted the Holy Spirit to work within me, giving me the power to live a victorious Christian life. I was chasing after God knowing He wanted to develop a new level of intimacy between us. He wants to do the same for everyone.

When I would open my Bible, I always asked for wisdom and understanding before I would start to read. The Bible was coming alive to me. How could I possibly know God if I did not know His Word? It would be impossible for me to know how to function in the world as a disciple for Christ, leading people to a more intimate relationship with the Heavenly Father until I had a clearer understanding of God myself. I always enjoyed reading the New Testament, and now the Old Testament was just as enjoyable. It was history pertaining to the Father I had not understood very well in the past. I was learning something new every time I opened the Bible to read, and I longed to learn more about the Father. I was no longer satisfied with what I knew about God. I had to *know* God and know what He was doing right now as well and in the past.

My life became sidetracked by many other things, and now God was after my full attention. As I learned to listen to His voice and seek His will and plans for me, I started realizing how I had quenched the Holy Spirit many times by allowing Him to only have the amount of control I was willing to give up. For the first time I was willing to relinquish all control and allow the master to take over. 2 Chronicles 7:14 says, "If my people, who are called by my name, will humble themselves and pray and seek my face and turn from their wicked ways, then I will hear from heaven and will forgive their sin and heal their land." I was one of His people. I had humbled myself, was praying and seeking the face of God. I was willing to turn from my wicked ways, so my Father heard me, forgave me, and now He was able to control areas of my life I had held onto so tightly.

Once I relinquished my control, I was convicted to allow God to have full control of my business. As soon as I allowed God to be in control, I started receiving blessing after blessing. I was listing homes one after the other, and they were selling rapidly. At every appointment I found myself taking more time to tell the clients about God, and I was talking very little about the real estate market. There was always an open door to share a personal testimony, and I continued to learn how to recognize them, walk through them, and usher Jesus in with me. I was being encouraged daily through sharing the Father with others and having them share with me.

As people opened up and talked, I could see the pain. I could feel the emptiness many of them had. I recognized the down and out, the ones who did not feel loved, the people with no hope, and the ones whose lives were shattered. I met the sick and afflicted. You could tell if they felt rejected and needed a friend and so much more. This was the same way it was for Jesus as He journeyed throughout the land, ministering to many people in need. I could no longer pass them by. I had to give some light to these people, share words of encouragement, show love, be a friend, and share my Friend in whom they could find their hope, peace, comfort, and joy.

If Jesus had not taken time out of His day to minister to others, many of the stories we read in the New Testament would not be there. Jesus took time to attend the wedding at Cana, and when the wine was gone He filled six stone water jars with the finest wine. Jesus took time to teach Nicodemus. Jesus stopped to talk to the Samaritan woman at the well and explain things to her. When Jesus went to Jerusalem for the feast of the Jews, He stopped to heal an invalid of thirty-eight years at the Sheep Gate. When the crowd followed Jesus to the far shore of the Sea of Galilee, He took time to bless the five barley loaves and two small fish and feed the estimated five thousand people (not to mention the twelve baskets of food left over). Jesus took time to teach and instruct the twelve disciples. He spent day after day with them investing in their lives. The list goes on and on of the times Jesus spent time ministering to others. I wonder what our world would be like if we took other people's lives as seriously as Jesus did? What would it be like if we were willing to invest in the lives of others and allow God to work through us? What a difference it would make. I reached a point in my life that I wanted to invest time in people, so I looked for the opportunities. We live in a society where people are so concerned about themselves that the needs of others often go unnoticed. We have become a selfish society of people who claim they care but do not have many actions to back it up.

One day I met with a young woman who had been married for less than two years. She had a baby girl and was expecting another child. Ready to walk out on her marriage, she had no idea where to go or which way to turn. She dearly loved her husband, but she realized she had turned away from God. She hated who she had become. Before meeting her husband and getting married, she was very involved in church, had an intimate relationship with God, and used her beautiful voice to sing for the Lord. She had not married a Christian husband, and instead of her leading by example and allowing him to see Christ in her, she found herself getting angry, lashing out with unkind words, using her voice for slander instead of praises, and spiraling downhill in her own relationship with God. She felt so unworthy of God's love and forgiveness. She poured out her heart to me, weeping like a baby. It was beyond her imagination to think the Heavenly Father would hold her in His arms, forgive her, comfort her, and give her another chance.

Talking for quite some time, I kept pouring out words of encouragement, claiming promises from the Bible, quoting scripture, and expressing the unconditional love of the Father to this young lady. We discussed God's plan for her marriage, her responsibilities as a wife, and the freedom she could experience if she was willing to humble herself and return to the Father. There was nothing that could separate her from the Father unless she continued to allow it. We cried and prayed together as this beautiful young lady poured out her heart to God for forgiveness, asked for restoration, and pleaded for His guidance to develop her into a woman after the Father's heart once again. She left my office with a new commitment to seek the face of God and allow Him to change her instead of trying to change others in her life.

Hours later, she came back to the office with her husband, bursting forth with excitement. During the time she had come to me for counsel, her husband went to a pastor to seek counsel as well. The Father was orchestrating a beautiful life change for each of them without the other even being aware. He created these two; He knows why He created them, along with what is best for them. Now the choice would be up to them. The three of us sat together talking, and they both made new commitments to each other, committing to put forth an effort toward making the marriage successful with God as the head of the house. As they held hands, I could see the sparkle of love in their eyes, and they humbly apologized to each other and took responsibility for their own actions. They agreed to find a church, find Christian friends to mentor them, and build a relationship with God and each other. After I prayed, they left my office and promised to come back and tell me the outcome as transformation in their marriage took place.

Several months later, they came by the office again just to let me know the marriage was healing and they were building a relationship with God. Then just over one year later, I received a call from them informing me that the husband was going to college and taking Bible classes. They wanted to come by and show me their beautiful baby boy and share what God was doing in their lives. Upon their arrival, I was handed a brochure for a youth ministry, and as I glanced down at the paper, there was his name in bold print. He had become the leader of the youth ministry and was touching lives all over the county. I praised God over and over again, thanking Him for sending this lovely couple my way and for giving me ears to hear the encouraging words the Holy Spirit guided me to say when they came by my office.

Sharing the love of Christ and what He has to offer people had become so important to me that I asked God for at least one divine appointment every day. Not wanting one day to go by without sharing Christ with someone, I looked for every opportunity I could. Even though others were receiving a blessing, the blessings I felt were even greater. My Father was teaching me to be bold. He wanted me to brag about Him just like I did my dad. He wanted me to think like Him, act like Him, and allow Him to be in full control. Reflecting back to when I was a toddler, I remember telling other kids who my father was. I would brag about him like he was the greatest hero that ever existed. Our Heavenly Father deserves to be praised and lifted up as the greatest hero that ever existed—because He is. He can do far greater things than any superhero portrayed. He is always there to rescue us and help us get back in the right direction. He can turn your life around. Be proud of Him, and let Him be proud of you.

I knew a significant turning point in my life was taking place right at that time. I was learning to walk with God and plant His Word in my heart. I could feel the presence of God in my life every day—and He wants you to experience the same. Recognizing that God was holding me in His arms and nurturing me reminded me of the times I would sit on my father's lap and he would hold me in his arms, reading a book to me, teaching me, challenging me, giving me instructions, and sometimes giving me messages to take to my brothers or sister. My dad was a prime example of what the Heavenly Father was now doing as He taught me daily, and I continued to mature.

I remember some of the specific times when my dad would give me a message to take to someone. I had no idea what it was about; I could not explain it, so I just made the delivery. Now I was experiencing times when the Heavenly Father gave me messages to take to others as well—some of which made no sense to me. Others I understood. I simple played the part of the messenger without questioning the intent.

Returning to Him with my whole heart, I hated the fact that I had ever drifted away from Him. As a young adult, I drifted away from my father—at times seeking my own independence—and I had done the same thing to my Heavenly Father. My stomach was churning inside at the thought of not remaining extremely close to both of them at all times. Their love for me never changed. It was consistent—even when I let them down, when I was disobedient, and when I rejected it—but apparently my love had changed somewhat toward them at times during my life. By becoming distant, actions to back up my love for either of them were few. I could say I loved my dad and my Heavenly Father, but words without actions to back them up were worthless. The true love of a father is unconditional and consistent, and we need to return love the same way.

As a parent, I have experienced times when my daughters drifted away from me, seeking their own independence. I would struggle with the feeling of rejection, and watching them make mistakes was painful. Knowing that I had to let them go in order to learn from their mistakes did not make it any easier. I continuously had to give them to God, sit back, and love them unconditionally. Over and over again I would place them in the hands of God and then snatch them back. It was hard to allow distance in our relationship, knowing it was not what I wanted. How much harder it must be for God to allow distance to be put between you and Him. How His heart must ache when you withdraw from Him, make mistakes, and resist His love. Do your actions show your love for Him?

Now I was putting my feelings into actions and showing the love I had to my Heavenly Father. One evening while praising and honoring God, I experienced an encounter with the Holy Spirit. I could not seem to contain the tears flowing down my face, and I wasn't sure why. Many thoughts raced through my mind, and I could not focus on any one of them. I felt honored and yet humble. I felt sad but yet joyous. I felt loved beyond measure. I felt convicted yet accepted. I felt pride being laid aside. And I felt the Spirit flowing through me in a different way than I had ever experienced before. I don't think I could even begin to explain it in words. I was broken but could not have explained why if someone had asked me. I was in a daze centered in the presence of God. The Father was pouring out His Spirit upon me. Many of us are not taught how to recognize the power and presence of the Holy Spirit in our lives. Worst yet, we do not even know the nature and role of the Holy Spirit. God wants to pour out His Spirit upon you. He wants you to experience the filling of the Spirit of God and let His gifts automatically flow through you. "'And it shall be in the last days,' God says, 'that I will pour forth my Spirit on all mankind'" (Acts 2:17, NASB).

I opened my Bible like I do many times when I am looking for answers from the Father, and my eyes fell on the following verse: "You will make known to me the path of life; In Your presence is fullness of joy; in your right hand there are pleasures forever" (Ps. 16:11, NASB). I knew God was making known to me little by little the path He wanted me to take for Him. He was removing the veil over my face so I could clearly see. He was equipping me to be ready, willing, and able to continue following His plans for my life and turn from my own plans. I had found full joy by being back in the presence of God, and I was seeing pleasures every day. Wow! What a promise. In my right hand there are pleasures forever. My right hand is very close, so I don't have to go far to find pleasures in life. This was only the beginning. Then I glanced down, and my eyes fell on another great verse: "Keep me as the apple of your eye; hide me in the shadows of your wings" (Ps. 17:8, NASB). I prayed this verse back to God over and over again. I wanted to please my Father and be the apple of His eye. I had been the apple of my earthly father's eye and never wanted to disappoint him, and now I did not want to disappoint my Heavenly Father. I wanted Him to hover over me and keep me in the shadow of His wings. His protection was even more important than I had needed from my dad. I *was* the apple of the Father's eye, and I *was* protected under His wings. You can also be the apple of His eye and find protection in the shadow of His wings. God gave us His most precious gift, His Son, and after His Son went to be with His Father, the Holy Spirit was sent to live in us and guard, guide, and direct our life in all truth.

The Holy Spirit is one of the gifts you receive through faith once you are saved. John 16:7 says, "But I tell you the truth, it is to your advantage that I go away; for if I do not go away, the Helper will not come to you; but if I go, I will send him to you." I find it amazing Jesus saw it as an advantage for us to have the Holy Spirit rather than keep walking on earth teaching people Himself. Still, many people do not even realize the importance of the Holy Spirit. The Holy Spirit guides your entire life if you allow Him. The Holy Spirit convicts you and guides you in the way of righteousness. He is the teacher of all things. The Spirit makes known to us the heart of the Father and even tells us the things of the future (John 16:5–15). The Holy Spirit also has many gifts He wants to give the Father's children. He has unique and special gifts for everyone. You need to be ready to accept the gift, open up the package, and put it to use (1 Cor. 12:4–11).

The Holy Spirit is so important in your Christian walk that the Bible warns us not to grieve the Holy Spirit of God, not to quench the Holy Spirit, and not to be stiff-necked (always rejecting the Holy Spirit). Instead, you need to be dependent on the Holy Spirit, allowing Him to be your guide, your counselor, and trainer in righteousness. The Spirit tends to be the most overlooked part of the Three in One: the Father, the Son, and the Holy Spirit. It had been this way in my life in the past, and now I was acknowledging His part in my life. I was experiencing His power in many new ways. I was growing in my knowledge and understanding. The Holy Spirit was definitely guiding me, teaching me, and training me in righteousness.

I started journaling every day because so much was happening and so many thoughts were running through my mind. I wanted to be sure I could read back and be reminded of the powerful things my Father was teaching me and telling me. When I read the Bible, I wanted to jot down all the new things He was revealing to me. When I prayed and then spent quiet time listening to His voice, I wanted to remember what He told me.

One day while spending time with God, I received a beautiful message: "Faith, you just have to be still and know that I am God. Stay humble before Me. Praise, honor, and adore Me. Continue to seek My guidance, and give Me all the glory. Never be boastful or haughty, and stay focused on My plan so the devil won't enter in and distract you. It is time to soak up My divine love for you and savor every minute of it—time to rejoice and be glad. It is time to feel My presence all around you—time to let the Spirit intercede for you since He always knows what to ask. You are experiencing moments with Me to cherish forever." After writing this down in my journal, I sat crying. The Heavenly Father was giving me instructions and guidance, just like my daddy had done for forty-six years. If you are willing to listen, the Father will communicate and instruct you as well.

God has a variety of creative and personal ways He still communicates with us. I know from experience that He still speaks through dreams, visions, His Word, other people, prophecies, and He will even speak directly into your mind. Are you willing to stand by His side and listen to His instructions? I stood by my father's side until the very end, listening to all he had to say—and now it was time to heed all the instructions from God.

Study Questions

If you are a believer in Christ, are you also a follower? Do you listen to the Spirit and follow knowing He is the Spirit of Truth?

Do you dedicate time to reading God's Word and getting to know Him?

Have you relinquished control over your life, giving God full control?

Do you always question "What's in it for me?" Or do you take time for others and show you care?

Do you look for divine appointments in your day-to-day journey? Are you seeking for opportunities to share Jesus Christ or just waiting for the opportunity to fall into place?

Do you have the Word of God planted within so you can share it when needed?

Do your actions and behavior show God you love Him?

Do you take time to be still and listen to God? Do you take His instructions seriously?

Ephesians 4:30 says, "And do not grieve the Holy Spirit of God, with whom you were sealed for the day of redemption." Do you grieve the Holy Spirit in any way?

1 Thessalonians 5:19–22 says, "Do not quench the Spirit. Do not despise prophetic utterances. But examine everything carefully; hold fast to that which is good; abstain from every form of evil." Do you quench the Holy Spirit?

Do you listen to prophetic words?

Do you examine everything carefully, holding on to everything good?

Do you stay away from every form of evil?

6

Following Instructions

Resting in the wilderness one day, I realized my focus in life had completely changed. My new focus was toward following the instructions in Colossians 3:17: "Whatsoever you do in word or deed, do all in the name of the Lord Jesus." With every thought or impression I received, I would ask if it could bring glory to God. My focus had turned toward the Father instead of myself. Jesus set the perfect example for us to follow by keeping His focus on His Father. In John 5:19, Jesus says, "Truly, Truly, I say to you, the Son can do nothing of Himself, unless it is something He sees the Father doing; for whatever the Father does, these things the Son also does in like manner." Growing up, I focused on my father over and over again to learn from him. Even as a toddler, I remember watching what he did and then trying to do it as well. I remember listening to him talk on the telephone and pretending I was holding a phone and talking away although I had no one to listen or respond. The many things I learned to do by following the instructions of both my mother and my father were priceless. Is there any doubt that Proverbs 1:8 is true? "Hear, my son, your father's instruction and do not forsake your mother's teaching." While I realize not all parents properly instruct their children, I was blessed to have godly parents who did their best to properly instruct me. They led by example—the best instruction I could have been given. It was like a life manual before me daily.

One of the things always fun to do was to get a few of my brothers and my sister together, and we would have church. One of us would lead singing, one would preach the message, and one would take up the offering as we had a church service. My brother, who always was the preacher, ended up being a preacher as an adult. He did what he saw his dad do and has reached many lives for Christ. This is the same thing that will happen in your life if you watch the Heavenly Father, listen to Him, and read the Bible. You see the attributes of Jesus and the Heavenly Father. Then you will look and act more and more like Him every day.

The Father gives many instructions throughout the Bible. As you read, it is important to stay focused and remove everything that could distract you. Whether you are a son or a daughter, the Father has many instructions for you to follow, and you need to listen. Spend time looking and listening for His instructions and be ready to accept them. Be sure you are focused on the lesson He is trying to teach you. If you are His child, you will want to please Him.

Imagine what would have happened if Abraham did not follow the instructions to separate himself from his old associates and go to a new country. He was promised divine favor, great prosperity, and that he would become a blessing to all families of the earth. When the earth was filled with violence, God revealed to Noah that there was going to be a great flood that would destroy man from the face of the earth. What if he had not built the ark as instructed? Noah found favor in the eyes of God, and we can too. Psalm 147:11 tells us, "The Lord takes pleasure in them that fear him."

We need to be praying for the fear of the Lord to be upon us. Psalm 86:11 says, "Teach me Your way, O Lord; I will walk in Your truth; Unite my heart to fear Your name."

We need to exhibit the fear of the Lord in our lives. Colossians 3:22 says, "Slaves, obey your earthly masters in everything; and do it, not only when their eye is on you and to curry their favor, but with sincerity of heart and reverence for the Lord." The very reason for our hope should be easily and readily explained to anyone, letting them know our hope is found in the gentleness and fear of Christ our Lord. We need to learn to fear the Lord our God constantly and not waiver from it. Proverbs 23:17

says, "Do not let your heart envy sinners, but live in the fear of the LORD always." It is important for us to teach others to fear the Lord so they want to follow His instructions. "Come, you children, listen to me; I will teach you the fear of the Lord" (Ps. 34:11, NASB).

We need to constantly let the fear of the Lord fall upon us so we walk in righteousness and do all things wholeheartedly because our desire is to be faithful to Him. In Psalm 111:10 we are told the fear of the Lord is the beginning of wisdom. Proverbs 1:7 tells us the fear of the Lord is the beginning of knowledge and only foolish people despise wisdom and knowledge. Throughout Psalms and Proverbs we are told the fear of the Lord is clean and enduring forever. The fear of the Lord prolongs life, and in the fear of the Lord we can have strong confidence. If fearing the Lord is a fountain of life aiding us to avoid the snares of death, who would not want to fear the Lord and follow His instructions?

By following the instructions from God, Noah took the warning seriously and started to construct the ark. Consider the magnitude of the work performed over the years as he built this immense boat. Surrounded by unbelievers who laughed at him and scoffed at his work, he maintained his faith and continued to build the ark year after year. When it was time to enter the ark, Noah experienced the wondrous work of God. Pairs of every animal, beast, fowl, and creature on earth lined up and entered into the ark. The mighty hand of the Lord was upon Noah, and it will be for each of you who are willing to follow the instructions of God. If Noah had not been obedient to the instructions, the world would have been wiped out, and we would not be here ourselves today. What a powerful example of following the Lord's instructions.

Another person who was willing to follow God's instructions was Moses. He was called to leadership, made excuses, but still obeyed knowing he had God's divine help. It was no easy task to follow the step-by-step instructions to lead the Israelites out of Egypt and through the wilderness. When people rebelled and complained along the journey, Moses became extremely frustrated, even to the point he disobeyed God's instruction and struck the rock God provided for water. Although

Moses never entered into the land God gave the Israelites because of his lack of trust in God, he saved the Israelite nation. From the beginning of the Bible to the end, there is story after story of people following the instructions the Heavenly Father gave them.

Trying to be more obedient to your Father's instructions is priceless. When you are following His instructions, you find treasures every day. I was finding gems I would cherish for a lifetime. The more we follow His instructions, the easier it is to put the puzzle of life together. We allow ourselves to see our Father's mighty hand at work in us. Following His instructions keeps us at peace with our Father. He will keep us in perfect peace when our eyes are fixed on Him. Are your eyes fixed on Jesus? You need to turn your attention away from what is bugging—away from what seems impossible and away from what is frustrating you. If something in your life is consuming your attention, deliberately turn away from it. Keep turning until your attention is fully focused on Jesus Christ. What loss would the kingdom of God suffer if you did not follow the Heavenly Father's instructions for your life? We are all called to do something for the kingdom. It is important that we listen and do our part.

To fix your eyes on Jesus, you have to intentionally set your gaze upon Him and watch intently. If you are facing difficult times and seasons in your life, you must fix your gaze on Him, and He will walk with you through the situation, whatever it may be. Once you have focused on Jesus Christ, it is much easier to walk faithfully with Him.

With your eyes focused on Him, the Father can give you instructions at the oddest times. It would be in the quiet times when He could get my attention. He has a pattern of waking me up around 3:00 a.m. every morning and keeping me awake for approximately one hour. Some nights I would get up, read the Bible and let the Spirit speak to me through the Word. Other nights I would just lie in bed, praying and worshipping God. There is something so special every night I wake up that I miss the nights I sleep straight through. This had become my private time with the Father, and I looked forward to it like I loved the private time I had with my dad. It was in the private times with no one interrupting that I could learn the most. I had His full attention, and He had mine. Do you take time in private to give God your full attention?

I often think of the story in Mark 8:22–26 where Jesus had entered the city of Bethsaida. When they came to Bethsaida, someone brought a blind man to Jesus and implored Jesus to touch him. Jesus took the blind man by the hand and led him out of the village. After they got out of the village, where all the things and people could not distract him, Jesus spit on his eyes and laid hands on him. When He asked him, "What do you see?" he replied, "I see men walking around, and they all look like trees." After this response, Jesus laid His hands on his eyes once again, and he could clearly see.

Jesus could have touched the man and healed him right there in the city, but I find it amazing that Jesus took him away where they could just be together one on one. Jesus could have restored his vision with the first touch, yet He waited and gave him a second touch before He could clearly see. We can all use a second touch of Jesus! When we think we have enough, have done enough, or have a good enough relationship with Jesus, that is when we need to come to Him for another touch so we can clearly see He has much more to offer us.

Like many Christians, I had spent many years being partially blinded. I could see many professing Christians looking just like others in the world. The believers and the nonbelievers all looked the same in many ways. When the blind man's vision was partially restored, he merely saw men, and they all looked the same—just like trees. When the man's vision was only partially restored, he did not start complaining to Jesus. He simply answered His question. I think he was probably excited just to be able to see something rather than nothing. How many of us complain about where we are rather than seeking another touch from Jesus? When our eyes are wide open, we are able to see the hungry, the poor, the sick, the down and out, the hurting, the homeless, and the broken and destitute people.

There were many other times when people came to Jesus believing they would be healed. In Matthew 8, Jesus healed the man with leprosy and Mary. In the next chapter, Jesus healed the sick woman, raised a dead girl to life, and restored a blind man's sight.

The Father told me, "Nothing will be impossible for you." Matthew 17:20–21 says, "Because you have so little faith, I tell you the truth, if you have faith as small as a mustard seed, you can say to this mountain, 'Move from here to there,' and it will move. Nothing will be impossible for you." My faith was increasing but was small as a mustard seed (or maybe even smaller). I knew nothing was impossible with God, but I had not personally experienced something as powerful as moving a mountain. My experiences up until now were small: Coming upon an accident and realizing it could have been me if I had been there two minutes earlier, seeing money just show up when there was a need, finding my tire flat in the driveway instead of having it happen while I was traveling down the interstate, or having surgery and the doctor taking necessary steps to correct my problem. I started praying for the power through Christ to move mountains. If this type of power was available for believers, I wanted to experience it.

It wasn't long before I experienced a taste of this power. I was preparing to see a doctor and schedule surgery for three herniated disks in my lower back. I expressed to my husband that I could no longer take the pain, and I just needed to get the surgery. I shared this with him before I retired the evening before my appointment. After I went to sleep, the Great Physician showed up in my bedroom; I began to talk in my sleep and have a discussion with God while my husband lay there awake—wondering what was going on as he listened to a one-sided conversation. I was asked if I believed God could heal me and repair the problem. I sat up in my bed and replied yes. I was then asked if I had enough faith to lay hands on my own back and ask Him to heal it. Thinking for a moment, I merely said, "I don't know." I had no idea why I had not put my faith into action and prayed for my own healing. I was then instructed to reach around, put my hands on my lower back, and ask Him to heal it. He told me that fancy words are not necessary; just ask, believing, and it will be done. While still sitting on the bed, I touched my back and said, "Lord,

I believe you can heal it." Lying back down, I felt the steps of surgery taking place—my back was being jerked into place, and my sciatic nerve was being repaired. Now I know it did not actually happen like it would if I was cut open on the operating table, but I could feel something being done step by step. I could fully describe the entire process.

Suddenly awakened, I turned to my husband and said, "My back was healed; the Great Physician was here and repaired my back." He then understood what had happened as I talked in my sleep and jerked around in the bed. It is now over seven years later, and I have had no problems with my back. I now understood that if we have faith, we can move mountains. This was a mountain-moving experience for me, and I am praying I experience many more of them. If Jesus is the example we are to live by and He was able to heal, we too can tap into the power through Jesus Christ and see people be healed. In John 14:12 Jesus instructs us, "He who believes in Me, the works that I do, he will do also; and greater works than these he will do; because I go to the Father." If you want to look like Jesus, you have to crave more of the Father's attributes. If you are His son or daughter, then why not have some of the same gifts He gave His son, Jesus? Jesus healed the sick, cast out demons, gave sight to the blind, raised the dead, and performed many more miracles. Why not look like you are related to Jesus? If you want the gifts Jesus has to offer you—like I did—you have to ask, seek, and you will find them. Diligently start searching for all the gifts and treasures He has for you.

Study Questions

Is your relationship with the Heavenly Father growing? Do you look more and more like Jesus as time passes?

What changes and actions would be necessary to develop a heart like Jesus?

Is your goal to please God? Or are you holding on to pride, seeking self-pleasure?

Like Noah, God may ask you to do something that seems really out of the ordinary. It may cause you to be laughed at, mocked, or persecuted. Would you do it regardless of the outcome?

What loss would the Kingdom of God suffer if you avoided following the Father's instructions for your life?

Do you take private, one-on-one time with God?

Are you at a stale position in your life where a second touch of Jesus could open your eyes to grow even closer to Him?

Do you complain a lot about where you are and what you are going through instead of asking Jesus to touch you once again with a refreshing new touch?

7

Prayer in the Wilderness

In the wilderness, I learned how to develop a more powerful prayer life. I found instructions throughout the Bible that taught me how to correctly pray so I could be closer to the Father. If spending time with God and talking to Him was the method to get to know Him, I wanted to try. The more I would humble myself before the Lord, the closer my relationship with Him grew. Humbling yourself before God is a way to show Him you honor Him.

In Matthew 6:5–8 we are told not to pray like the hypocrites, who stand on the street corners and in the synagogues to be seen, but to go into our inner room and close our door to pray to our Father, who is in secret. Then our Father, who sees what we do in secret, will reward us. It is important to set aside a time and a place to get alone with God and pray. Even Jesus went to a secluded place to pray at times. He needed time alone to communicate with His Father. In Mark 1:35 we are told, "In the early morning, when it was still dark, Jesus got up, left the house, and went to a secluded place to pray, and was praying there." If even Jesus needed a place of seclusion to spend time with God, why would you think you don't? Again in Luke 5:16 we read, "Jesus Himself would often slip away to the wilderness and pray." Jesus needed time alone with His Father, and so do you. I think of how precious time was when I could be alone with my father. We could talk, share our innermost secrets, laugh, and just enjoy being in the presence of each other. Time alone with the Heavenly Father is of even greater importance. I was learning to talk, share what

I thought to be my innermost secrets (even though He already knew), laugh, cry, and just enjoy being in the presence of my Father.

We all need time alone with God, and prayer is our way of communicating with God and sharing in conversation with Him. Check your attitude before prayer and come to God with the proper attitude. Do not pray just to say you did it, but do it with a heart desiring to spend time with God in an intimate way.

We are also told not to use meaningless repetitious words just to have something to say. The Father knows everything you need before you even ask Him. He knows your struggles and sins. He knows every aspect of your life. He knows how you feel. He wants you to come asking His will be done—not yours. He is not concerned that we have a beautifully written script of words to recite; He would rather hear us simply talk to Him telling Him what is in our heart in the same way you would talk to your best friend or spouse. He loves and cares for you without limitations. He is fair and seeks to heal and save all of us if we have faith and follow in His will. He is love and mercy. Simply open up and talk to your Father.

Then Jesus goes on to give us instructions on how we should pray in verses 9–13: "Our Father who is in heaven, Hallowed be your name. Your kingdom come, Your will be done, on earth as it is in heaven. Give us this day our daily bread. And forgive us our debts, as we forgive our debtors. And lead us not into temptation, but deliver us from evil. For Yours is the kingdom and the power and the glory forever. Amen."

I had recited this prayer many times in my life without really looking at its meaning, as I am sure many of you have done. I could not even explain what it fully meant. I started realizing the prayer was designed as a pattern rather than a chant repeatedly prayed. Jesus intended for each part of the Lord's Prayer to teach us something about God, our needs, and prayer itself.

Our Father in Heaven. First, I learned the value of recognizing I was praying to God Almighty, Himself. I learned to approach Him as a child just like I would approach my loving father. I approached my father with humility and love. But often I have approached my Heavenly Father like

He was just there to hear my needs and requests. I learned the importance of humbly recognizing at the onset of my prayers who God is.

Hallowed be your name. If you look up the definition of *hallowed*, you will see it means "to demonstrate as holy" or "to honor as holy." Many recite the Lord's Prayer without even giving much thought to what we are really saying in the segment. Once I realized that I was really praying to God to show me how holy and perfect He was, I was able to move on and recognize His holiness in a greater way. I could feel His closeness just like I could feel my father's, and I found this comforting. My father always took charge, and this left me feeling safe and secure. I trusted in His judgment and authority. If I truly believe the Heavenly Father is Sovereign, I have to accept He is in charge of everything. This is what I had always been saying when I quoted *"Your kingdom come, your will be done on earth as it is in heaven."* If I wanted the Father's will, I wanted His desires to be done and was willing to submit to His authority. The only way the world around you will see evidence of His kingdom is if Jesus's people pray and obey God's will.

Give us this day our daily bread. While God does not give us everything we ask for, He does provide our needs. Each day you can trust He will provide your needs for that day, and He already knows everything you need tomorrow. The Father cares for His children and wants to take care of them. A good example is when God was leading the children of Israel out of Egypt. Every morning He provided manna from heaven and supplied just what they needed for that day. This forced the Israelites to continue relying on Him to provide. We have become so self-sufficient that we often forget to rely on God.

Forgive us our debts, as we forgive our debtors. Luke 11:4 says, "And forgive us our sins, for we ourselves also forgive everyone who is indebted to us." God is the only One who can forgive your sins. You must pray and confess your sins to God and admit you have a need to be forgiven. It is very significant every day that you rid yourself of any sin in your life causing separation between you and your Father. If you do not repent of your sin, then you are more likely to repeat it. *And lead us not into temptation but deliver us from evil.* Temptation is something no one can avoid on his own no matter how much self-control he has. Full dependency upon the Holy Spirit, who lives in Christians, is our only hope of recognizing temptation and escaping it.

The prayer is closed by declaring God's holiness and sovereignty. You are praying for God's kingdom, power, and glory to be lifted up and made beautiful in the eyes of everyone. By saying amen, we agree we truly believe that God has heard our prayer and that He will do it. A prayer offered in faith is answered. You need to believe if you ask. Believe and you will receive. "Therefore I say to you, all things for which you pray and ask, believe that you have received them, and they will be *granted* you" (Mark 11:24, NASB; emphasis added).

In the Bible we are told to pray that we may not be tempted. In 1 Thessalonians 5:17–18 we are instructed to pray without ceasing and to give thanks for everything. If prayer is your way of communicating with God and building an intimate relationship with Him, not only do you need to spend private time with God, you need to spend time listening to Him for answers and hearing His instructions. Refrain from asking with wrong motives. "You ask and do not receive, because you ask with wrong motives, so that you may spend it on your pleasures" (James 4:3, NASB). I have spent a lot of time on my own pleasures in the past. Now I have to refocus and spend time on the pleasures of the Kingdom. If you ask for things from the Heavenly Father with wrong motives, you should not be surprised when you don't get them; however, when you ask with proper motives, stand guard and look for results. This principle covers a much broader area than just things of monetary value. It includes everything you ask the Father. When you pray, always ask yourself whether your request is going to bring glory to God or not. "If you abide in Me, and My words abide in you, ask whatever you wish, and it will be done for you" (John 15:7, NASB).

Life in the wilderness can get lonely if you are in the wilderness without God. I wonder how people go through all the trials they face in life without Jesus. While spending time alone trying to deal with the loss of my earthly father, I found a fresh desire to abide in Him and have His words abide in me. If I was abiding in Him, I would not ask for things with wrong motives. My motives would result in bringing glory to God, so in the end He could say, "Well done, good and faithful servant." Are you abiding in the presence of Jesus and allowing His Word to abide in you? If not, it is time to lay everything else aside. Do not let anything stand between you and the Father.

I knew sin was disobedience to God and it could separate me from Him. So daily repentance became a necessity. The Holy Spirit will not dwell in an unclean temple. My goal was to remain yielded to the will and grace of God and to be filled with the Holy Spirit. I felt a greater forgiveness as I let go and truly forgave others. "Whenever you stand praying, forgive, if you have anything against anyone, so that your Father who is in heaven will also forgive you your transgressions" (Mark 11:25, NASB). Become more pleasing in His eye by always forgiving, and it will come back to you as you pray for forgiveness.

When praying, it is important to "bless and curse not." Always seek goodwill for others in everything you say and do. Pray your enemies are blessed with good things whether you like it or not because it is a direct command from the Heavenly Father's Word.

Prayer is important to the spiritual lives of Christians. Many people profess to be Christian yet never spend time in prayer. Others stop praying because they say their prayers are never answered. Prayer is a tool greatly misapplied and many times underutilized. I was learning that to follow Christ I had to maintain reverence for God. I had to acknowledge Him as Creator of the universe and give Him the glory, praise, and honor He deserved. I had to recognize His rightful place in my life and thank Him for all the blessings He abundantly supplied. I was overcoming the unnecessary attitude of begging and pleading while knowing that God already knew what I needed and rightly desired. I was gaining boldness in thanking God before I saw the results to show Him how much I trusted Him.

Study Questions

Do you spend time on a regular basis with God in prayer? Do you have a place to get alone without interruptions?

Can you open up and share what is on your heart with God? Do you hold some things back thinking it does not matter or God does not care to hear about them?

Do you simply talk to your Father, or do you try to polish your words to perfection?

Do you go to your Father with the right attitude?

Do you pray blessings for those who have hurt you? Think for a minute of people you would consider your enemies: people you do not like or maybe hold grudges against. Write down their names. Spend time praying blessings upon them, and ask the Father to help you forgive them in your heart so you mean what you pray.

Matthew 21:22 says, "And all things you ask in prayer, believing, you will receive." If the only limitations you have on prayer is to ask, believe, and receive, which one of the three are keeping you from having what you need and desire from your Father? It may be a different one of the three on various occasions. What steps can you take to be sure all three of these limitations are set in to action so you see results? This may be a good time to start a prayer journal if you are not doing so.

8

Fasting in the Wilderness

Further down in Matthew 6 we read privacy is important when we fast and pray. The Father does not like proud people who try to be noticed for what they do. When you fast, you are not to put on a gloomy face and neglect your appearance so that you will be noticed by men. You are to anoint your head and wash your face so that your fasting will not be noticed by men but by your Father who sees what is done in secret. Then He will reward you. You need to discipline yourself to fast, make a sacrifice, and spend time with God.

Fasting is the most powerful spiritual discipline of all the spiritual disciplines. When you fast and pray, the Holy Spirit is able to transform your life and work on a much larger scale than you can imagine. If you fast with proper biblical motives, seeking God's face, I believe God hears from heaven and will answer your prayers. He will heal your life, your church, your community, and our nation. You need to fast with a broken, repenting spirit seeking a change in your life and intercede for others in the world. Remember when you fast that you are humbling yourself before God and glorifying Him. Power is released through each one of you when you fast and pray through the Holy Spirit.

Fasting is a spiritual discipline that has been ignored for a long time with most Christians. I wonder if it due to the lack of self-discipline or just not having enough knowledge. Regardless of the reason, fasting is important for an intimate relationship with the Heavenly Father. Fasting is a sacred time in which Christians abstain from a form of pleasure or food and focus their lives around God. It is important to have the right motives for fasting. Fasting is merely humbling yourself before God and glorifying Him. Spend time in prayer before you fast. Confess every sin and invite the Holy Spirit to lead your life. Be sure to let Jesus know your desire is to know Him more and build a more intimate relationship with the Father. Always acknowledge that Jesus died in your place on the cross for your sins. Avoid entering into a fast while holding grudges and being unforgiving of others. Pray against anger, pride, and envy so the enemy cannot use any of these things against you.

Fasting is a condition of the heart. Many effective ministers of God today and all the way back to the apostle Paul fast as part of their walk with God. Prepare your heart spiritually and prepare yourself physically before you start to fast for any length of time. Examine your heart and clear up any sin in your life that you have not confessed before God. The Bible tells us if you have wickedness in your heart, the Lord will not hear your prayers. So be sure to repent of your sins before expecting to be heard (Ps. 66:18, paraphrased). Avoid entering into a fast while harboring bitterness in your heart. Pray against anger, pride, and envy so the enemy cannot use any of these things against you.

Fasting allowed me to exchange the needs of my physical body for those of the spiritual body. It will do the same for you. While in the wilderness I realized just how much my spiritual body was suffering. While fasting, I gained spiritual insight and understanding of the Word of God. The Holy Spirit would guide me in truth, and my relationship with my Father grew. I learned that while refraining from food I had to replace it with long times of prayer and reading God's word. It brought me into more intimate communion with God, who aided me to complete my fast. The more time I spent with God, the more meaningful the fast became. While it is a good thing to share with friends and family the benefits of fasting, it is not good to brag about it to gain any personal recognition.

Let's take a look at the story of Esther. Once Esther was made queen, Mordecai became aware of Haman's plot to destroy the Jews. Mordecai persuaded Esther to help by going into the king's presence to beg for mercy and plead with him for her people. Esther agreed but sent instructions for Mordecai to gather all the Jews in Susa to fast and pray for her. She ordered them to not eat or drink anything for three days before she would go into the king's inner court. Esther and her maids also fasted along with the Jews.

The law stated that unless the king summoned people into his inner court, they were to be put to death if they entered. Esther's life was on the line. She trusted God would answer her prayers, along with the prayers of her people, after they went before the Lord with fasting and prayer. On the third day she put on her royal robes and entered the inner court of the palace to see the king. Esther went to the king and obtained favor in his sight. What an outcome: favor in the king's sight rather than being killed! The king asked what was troubling her and what her request was. Esther was so welcomed in the king's court that she was given freedom to ask whatever she wanted from the king. The king even offered up to half of the kingdom to her. She made her request, simply inviting him for dinner. You might think at this point, "How is this going to help the Jews?" After two banquets, Esther finally gave her request to the king asking that her life be spared and also the lives of her people. The fasting and prayer paid off when Esther saved her people in the end. I know when we go to the King of kings He is ready to hear our requests and grant them for us. He simply wants us to come into the inner court and spend time with Him. When people take intimate time with the Father by fasting, praying, and seeking His face for help and instruction, results happen.

There are many other references to fasting in the Bible that date all the way back to ancient time. In Jonah 3 we are told how the city of Nineveh reacted to Jonah's message from God. According to verse 5, "all the people proclaimed a fast and put on sackcloth from the greatest of them even to the least of them." Further down in verse 7 the king himself "issued a proclamation and it said, In Nineveh by the decree of the king and his nobles: Do not let man, beast, herd, or flock taste a thing. Do not let them eat or drink water." They were instructed to call on God earnestly and turn from their wicked way. In Leviticus 23:27–29 the Israelites were commanded to "afflict their bodies" on the Day of Atonement, which is referred to as "the fast" in Acts 27:9. It is recorded that Moses fasted twice for a forty-day period.

There is an amazing story in Daniel 6 pertaining to fasting. Daniel, a man of God, was one of the three administrators of over one hundred twenty satraps. The satraps were accountable to the administrators so the king would not suffer any loss. The king was so pleased with the exceptional qualities Daniel possessed that he planned to set him over the entire kingdom. Jealousy raged among the commissioners and satraps, and they began to look for a way to bring him down. They could find no fault in Daniel. He was trustworthy. He handled government affairs properly. He was neither corrupt nor negligent in any way. They got together and devised a plan to use his devotion to God against him. They plotted to go to the king to encourage him to sign an injunction stating if anyone worshiped any God or man besides the king himself for the next thirty days, he would be thrown into the lion's den.

After the injunction was signed, Daniel continued to kneel three times a day praying and giving thanks before God. The men went to the king and reported what Daniel was doing and reminded the king that he could not change any edict or decree he had issued. The king tried to think if there was any way he could avoid having Daniel thrown into the lion's den. He liked Daniel and it bothered him greatly to have to fulfill this command. With no way out, the king issued the order and told Daniel, "Your God whom you constantly serve will Himself deliver you."

The king, in his great distress, went off to the palace and spent the night fasting. At dawn the next day he hurried off to the lion's den and called out to Daniel in a troubled voice: "Daniel servant of the living God, has your God whom you constantly serve been able to deliver you from the lions?" Wow! Fasting paid off. Daniel was alive because God sent His angel to shut the mouth of the lions. They did not harm Daniel in any way. If the power of fasting can shut the mouths of hungry lions, it can certainly destroy the strongholds of evil and usher in a great revival in your life and around the world.

During your time of fasting, worship the Heavenly Father and praise Him for His attributes. Meditate on His Word. Ask for His wisdom to gain understanding of its meaning and how you can incorporate it into your life. Always seek the Father's will when fasting and implore the Father to lead you to advance the Kingdom and spread His glory in the world. The purpose of fasting is to produce a transformation in your life and give you more focused attention and dependence upon the Heavenly Father. God will bless you for your commitment and fasting. Grab hold of the meaning of praying without ceasing. Bring your personal needs and the needs of others before the Heavenly Father. Center your entire being on Him and expect to encounter personal experiences with Him. You will only grow closer to Him when fasting, feel His presence, and experience His answers to your prayers. Joel 2:12 says, "'Yet even now,' declares the Lord, 'return to Me with all your heart and with fasting, weeping and mourning.'" It is time for Christians to return to God wholeheartedly—fasting, praying, and expecting results throughout our nation.

Study Questions

Have you ever set aside a time to fast?

When reading examples of stories from the Bible, can you recognize God's power in the outcome? Do you see the results?

Can you see any benefit in fasting for a period of time yourself?

Is your heart in the proper condition to fast?

9

The Treasure Chest

I started searching for the treasures and the gifts God wanted to share with me. In my search, the first treasure I found was a deeper meaning of trust. As a little girl, I remember my father holding out his arms for me to run and jump into them. I had to trust he would catch me. Then there was the day I started learning to ride a bicycle. He would run beside me while holding the bicycle up so I would not fall and get hurt. I had to trust he would not let go until I had my balance. If my father made a promise, I trusted he would stick by it. My relationship with my father required trust continuously, and yet I seemed to vaguely know the definition when it came to trusting my Heavenly Father.

I had taken trust for granted. It was comfortable and easy to accept the childlike concept because it was what I had experienced with my father. Minimal trust came easily with God—but not the deep, unexplainable trust. I never really put all my trust in God, never trusted and leaned intently on His promises, and never put the kind of trust in Him that took the ordinary and expected the extraordinary—the unwavering trust in which you know everything will work out for the glory of God. Think for one moment about the level of trust the Israelites had when they were wandering in the desert for forty years. Their clothes never wore out, their sandals never wore out, and they ate no bread nor drank any wine. Yet enough manna fell from heaven to keep them from going hungry. They knew the Lord was their God, and they fully trusted in Him to deliver them into the Promised Land. Can you trust like the children of Israel did? If you don't know where your next meal will come from, can you trust Him to provide? If you can't see victory over the battles you are facing, can you put on the armor of God and trust that you will win? When you feel you have no one to turn to, will you turn to the Father and His Son, whom you can trust? Maybe you have allowed the pressures of the world to discourage you just like I had done—the pressures that leave you feeling exhausted. The Father wants you to know He is with you, and He will never leave you. I started observing that no matter what the situation, I could trust Him to lead me and guide right then. The Father was so close to me that I could draw my strength from Him. So can you. His peace will flow through you like a river running downstream. I had discovered a better understanding of the word *trust*. The *Encarta* dictionary describes *trust* as "confidence in and reliance on good qualities, especially fairness, truth, honor, or ability." To be trustworthy, you are expected to behave responsibly and honorably. Jesus displayed all these qualities and devoted Himself to trusting the Father. If Jesus could trust the Father, so can we. The psalmist says, "In God I put my trust; I shall not be afraid" (Ps. 56:4, NASB). Trusting is a conscious decision each person must make. God can be trusted totally and exclusively. We have to acknowledge and know His presence in order to trust Him and not be afraid. We can share all He is and all He has if we just learn to trust Him.

The second treasure I found was peace. Living with my father, I had peace in many ways. I had peace of mind knowing I would not go hungry, knowing I would have clothes to wear and I would have a place to live. It was peaceful knowing I belonged to a family and I had a father who would protect me. I had the peace of knowing his love for my mother was secure and they were committed to staying together.

But I needed a peace of heart and mind. I needed peace that wasn't fragile and could not be taken away. I needed "a heart at peace that gives life to the body" (Prov. 14:30). I found peace so deep within that nothing or no one could touch it. It is a peace only the Father can give—a peace I had not possessed in the past. "For He himself is our peace" (Eph. 2:14,

NASB). If you know Jesus, you can have peace, for Jesus is the Prince of Peace.

Later I stumbled on guidance. When you are little, you like guidance from your father. You know and accept it as a way of life. It is a gift you need in order to grow, learn, and reach maturity. Without it you would be confused and not know which way to turn. Then you reach an age where you think you are smart enough to guide yourself, so you reject your father's guidance. At this time in life, you probably know more than Dad—at least I thought I did. It is years later before you are willing to admit you were wrong. What child at the age of thirteen does not think he knows all there is to know and is smarter than his parents?

In this same way, we rebel against the guidance of the Heavenly Father. We think we know best; we think our knowledge is superior to the knowledge of the great King of kings. This is totally wrong. You must accept and admit He is the greatest guide you can follow at all times. He always knows best. He always knows the path you should take. He will guide you in His truth and teach you (Ps. 25:4–5). He will guide us with His counsel (Ps. 73:24). He will guide us always (Isa. 58:11). He will guide us in the ways of wisdom and down straight paths (Prov. 4:11). He will guide us to the end (Ps. 48:14). All of these are promises found in the Word of God, and I am claiming them. Look them up. Read them for yourself. Stand firm by claiming God's promises every day. With His perfect guidance, how can you go wrong?

I trusted my father's guidance since he was a smart man. He could accomplish anything he set his mind to do. He could repair about anything that broke down. You would find him in the driveway repairing the car, doing any carpentry work needing to be done around the house, or tearing down the washing machine and repairing it. I even remember a time when he took every little spring and piece out of his watch to see what was wrong and put every little piece back in place except one. And it started ticking even though one piece never found its place back in the watch. There was nothing my dad would not attempt to repair, and he did most of it successfully, avoiding the expense of repairmen. If he did not know how to do something, he would read and study until he figured it out. He was wise in his decision-making processes in business and finances. He had even greater wisdom in discerning and learning to preach and teach the word of God. I was only ten years old when I decided I wanted the wisdom and knowledge my father had. If someone asked me what I wanted to be when I grew up, I did not think in terms of a profession. I simply wanted to be a knowledgeable person like my dad.

Desiring my father's wisdom and knowledge wasn't enough. Although I did seem to inherit some of it, now I was gaining wisdom and knowledge through the Spirit of the Lord. Isaiah 11:2 says, "The Spirit of the Lord will rest on him—the Spirit of wisdom and of understanding, the Spirit of counsel and of power, the Spirit of knowledge and of the fear of the Lord."

We are ordered to get wisdom in Proverbs 4:7: "Wisdom is supreme; therefore get wisdom." I talked earlier in the book about asking for wisdom. God's Word says if we ask for wisdom, He will give it generously. So if you do not have wisdom, you have not asked for it. It is that simple. The Father wants us to have the wisdom that comes from heaven. "For the wisdom that comes from heaven is first of all pure, then peace-loving, considerate, submissive, full of mercy and good fruit, impartial and sincere" (James 3:17, NIV). Accepting that I lacked wisdom, I intended to keep this request on my prayer list. I wanted the wisdom that comes from heaven, and I wanted it in abundance. Since wisdom is a gift God will not withhold from anyone, I am going after it and taking as much as He is willing to give me.

We can also accept the treasure of knowledge. In 2 Peter 3:18 Peter tells us to grow in the grace and knowledge of our Lord and Savior, Jesus Christ. He desires for us to know all we can about him, and we must continually seek—never accepting that we have enough. In the book of Colossians, Paul was writing to encourage Christians at Laodicea. Paul wanted them to experience the full riches and complete understanding so they knew God's mystery, Christ Himself. In Colossians 2:3 Paul says that in Christ is the hidden treasure of wisdom and knowledge. So we know where the hidden treasure is. Yet we still stand back, reluctant to go and get it. If we knew there was gold buried in our backyard, would we dig it up? Sure we would. We would dig hole after hole until we found it. We would not run away and just forget all about it. We cannot accomplish all the Father's intended plans if we run from knowledge and wisdom. The value of this treasure cannot be overlooked; we have to dig deeper and deeper, searching for more of this treasure, studying the Word of God, and spending intimate time communicating with the Father. The more we read and learn, the more we realize we don't know. Be thankful that God is willing to increase your knowledge and wisdom if you continually seek it until you are in heaven with Him and all mysteries are unveiled. What a day of rejoicing that will be! If you are not asking for the gifts of wisdom and knowledge, it is time to start. With all the changes taking place in the world, you need all the wisdom you can get.

Increased wisdom gave me strength. When I was a toddler, I loved to play in the yard with my father. It was especially fun when he would grab my arms and spin me in circles so fast my feet came off the ground and I felt like I was flying. He would twirl me around and around until we both were so dizzy we could not stand up. He was so strong that he would do it over and over again, and his hands never slipped. Other times he would clasp his hands together and let me sit on them and swing me back and forth like his arms were the chains holding up a swing. I would see him arm wrestling with my brothers, and he could always take them down. In my childish eyes, he was like David standing up to the giant.

The Heavenly Father showed His strength in a different way. He had supernatural strength—strength He was willing to share and strength stronger than any man's. His strength would pick me up when I fell down. His strength would carry me through every storm, calm my spirit when I was troubled, pick up the heavy pile of burdens I tried to carry, and carry them for me. His strength would go the extra mile to get my attention and not give up on me. His desire was for me to have this same type of strength. He was willing to give it to me. "Yet those who wait for the Lord will gain new strength; they will mount up with wings like eagles, they will run and not get tired, they will walk and not become weary" (Isa. 40:31, NASB). I was waiting for my new strength, the strength only the Lord can give. Being joyful in the Lord was my first step toward gaining my new strength. The more excited I got about Him, the stronger I felt. I no longer had to fear, for He was with me. He was arming me with strength to accept my destiny and move forward as a disciple for Him. Choose to spend more time gaining strength from the Father instead of only strengthening yourself working out in a gym. Americans spend millions of dollars on gym equipment, gym memberships, and gym clothing. They work out for hours upon hours strengthening their physical stature but neglect their spiritual strength. The strength He will supply can conquer the enemy when you go into battle. In Isaiah 41:10 it says, "Do not fear, for I am with you; do not anxiously look about for I am your God. I will strengthen you, surely I will help you, surely I will uphold you with my righteous right hand." He was strengthening my heart, my soul, my mind, and my inner spirit, not building up my muscles. Mark 12:30 says, "Love the Lord your God with all your heart and with all your soul and with all your mind and with all your strength." How do you love the Lord with all your strength? You must love Him earnestly, love Him more than anyone else, love Him more than anything else, love Him more than yourself, and love Him with all the strength you can muster up within you. Don't you want to feel this great strength from your Father?

As I received strength from the Father, my courage began to grow as well. From the time I was four years old, I remember going swimming during the summer at a place called Manatee Springs. My father taught me how to swim as a toddler, so at the age of four I was already a pretty good swimmer. I would muster up the courage to jump into the cool spring water and try to swim from one end of the spring to the other. Bystanders thought it was amazing to see such a little girl swimming, so they stood around watching me. I would climb back out of the water smiling and dive or jump back in. Even though I knew there were lifeguards all around, it took all the courage I had because deep inside I was somewhat afraid of drowning. I covered up the fear really well so people would think I was brave. My dad would cheer me on, and I definitely did not want to disappoint him or any bystander.

Being the youngest of seven children, it took courage to go to school every year. It was impossible to get a teacher who had not already taught at least two of my siblings. The teachers had already formed an opinion of me, and I didn't even get a chance to be myself. I was the disruptive one, the troublemaker, the quiet one, or some other preconceived personality. It took courage to just show up and try to be me. Do you form an opinion of God before allowing Him to show you who He really is?

Courage was another treasure the Father was giving me. He was giving me courage to step out in faith, believing all things were possible through Him. He was giving me courage to stand firm in the faith. He was giving me courage to be bold and share the miraculous things He was doing in my life. I was even finding I had enough courage to trust the voice I thought was the Father speaking to me. Why should I fear? This loving Father promised He would never leave me. He would help me fight any battle I entered. "Be strong and courageous, do not be afraid or tremble at them, for the Lord your God is one who goes with you. He will never fail you or forsake you" (Deut. 31:6, NASB). You have nothing to fear. God is with you every step of the way every day of your life if you allow Him to be. "Be on your guard; stand firm in the faith; be men of courage; be strong" (1 Cor. 16:13, NIV). If you are spiritually strong, you will have courage.

David was merely a young lad when he had enough courage to fight Goliath. Everyone thought he was crazy wanting to go fight with a giant. Bystanders laughed as he went up against the giant with merely a sling and five little stones. He had all the courage he needed as he went forward with the strength of the Lord. What a shock to everyone watching as he put one little stone in his sling, hurled it at the giant, and knocked him right in the middle of his forehead. The giant fell to the ground and died. Is your courage strong enough to fight off Satan, or do you let him win the battle over and over again? If Satan is your giant, you need to courageously stand up against him and fight. You can win!

Once you become courageous in Christ, you find freedom. Freedom caught me off guard when I was seventeen years of age. My father let me have the freedom to make many decisions for myself. He gave me enough freedom to succeed or fail so I could learn from my decisions. My parents had bought a motel in Blowing Rock, North Carolina, in the middle of my senior year in high school. My father had to be prepared to open the motel by early spring, which meant I would change schools in the middle of my senior year. After many discussions, my father allowed me to make the choice to either stay behind with a friend and finish three months of school without them or move three months before them to Blowing Rock, North Carolina. This was the first major choice I remember making that could affect my life deeply. What if I made the wrong choice? I had been with my friends for years. Could I make new friends and feel accepted in such a short time? Where would I feel most comfortable alone for three months without my parents? I moved early, thinking it would be better to make some friends before graduation, and later realized by having the freedom to choose that I made the wrong decision. Graduation just did not feel right. There were no memories associated with the years I invested, and I longed to be at graduation with my friends in Florida. I never went to a class reunion because there were no bonds created in such a short time. What I worked twelve years to accomplish felt like nothing.

This is the same way the Heavenly Father operates. He gives us freedom to make our own choices. He tries to direct us, but the final decision is up to us. Will you give your life to Him? Will you serve Him wholeheartedly? Will you refrain from making the wrong decisions and keep your focus on Him? There are many decisions in serving the Lord Jesus Christ. You have to decide if you will put Him first in your life. Will you allow the Holy Spirit to convict you and guide your every step? Will you seek the face of your Father and strive to live a life here on earth like His Son, Jesus, did? Will you freely surrender everything you have to be used to the glory of God?

If you make the decision to allow the Holy Spirit to direct your life, then a different type of freedom takes place. 2 Corinthians 3:17 says,

"Now the Lord is the Spirit, and where the Spirit of the Lord is, there is freedom." This was the freedom I was now experiencing. I had freedom knowing the Spirit of the Lord was with me and directing my life. I had invited the Holy Spirit into my life to fill me. I was learning to remove myself and replace it with His Spirit. Are you experiencing this type of freedom? Do you have the Spirit of the Lord residing in you and giving you freedom? Does freedom reign in your heart?

When the Holy Spirit starts taking over, you have to deal with a lot of junk in your life. I have five brothers and one sister. We would consistently do things to annoy and aggravate each other knowing it was not the right thing to do. My father would make us go back and apologize when we did something to hurt or harm one another. He would never defend us when we were in the wrong with anyone. If we had done something wrong, apologizing was a requirement. He would go with us to be sure we followed through with the apology. He also taught us the importance of accepting an apology and forgiving one another. He impressed upon us not to hold grudges or try to take revenge. This taught me to take responsibility for my own actions.

Taking responsibility for my own actions is also important to God. I had to seek the treasure of forgiveness from some people and also forgive some people. Not completely knowing how I should go about this, I took the matter to the Lord in prayer. I petitioned Him to show me people to whom I needed to give an apology and those I needed to forgive. Just like a dad, He started showing me one by one when I needed forgiveness so I could experience more freedom. Apologizing was not as difficult as forgiving those who had harmed me and never asked for forgiveness. Some of the hurts were deeply rooted, and it was hard to weed them out. I started focusing on how much the Heavenly Father had to forgive me. I failed and messed up in so many ways over and over again; yet as soon as I asked for forgiveness, He erased my failures and mistakes as if they never had happened. If the one I love most could do this for me, I had to do the same to others. Matthew 6:14 instructed us to forgive men who sin against us, and then our Heavenly Father will forgive us. I had to forgive to be forgiven, and so do you. Colossians 3:13 says, "Forgive as the Lord forgave you." Just how does Jesus forgive you? He forgave completely, totally, with nothing held against you, and He remembers your sin no more. He holds no grudges and takes no revenge. That is the type of forgiveness He is willing to offer you.

Having a forgiving heart is one way we show obedience to God. Obeying my father was not always easy. I wanted to obey, but he made too many crazy rules and guidelines. How could he expect me to obey so many rules that left me feeling bound? I just knew he needed to lighten up a little and not make it so hard to obey. It was his fault because he made the rules too strict. I tried to obey all I could, but I know I failed at times. I worked extra hard at obedience because I wanted to please my dad. I hated it when I disappointed him.

Years had gone by since I focused on complete obedience to God. I lived a fairly good life, tried to do what was right, went to church, prayed, and tried to avoid disobeying His commands even though I failed at times. Obedience comes naturally once you focus on Him. I was seeking His face and did not want Him to see any disobedience in me. I wanted to show Him the respect He deserved. I knew the secret to successfully obeying God was love. This was such a small word with a great big meaning. Without love, nothing else will fall into place in my spiritual walk. Mastering love allows us to love others the way Jesus loves us. Do you love your neighbor as much as you love yourself? I wanted Jesus to reveal Himself to me, dwell in me, and be my friend. Do you unconditionally love everyone, or are you selective with whom you will love? Do you want to be purified, living in continual peace and joy while experiencing the love of the Father? Can you even imagine how much the Heavenly Father loves you?

After dealing with forgiveness and being willing to be completely obedient (this doesn't mean I'm perfect, but that I'm striving toward perfection) God started to unveil the depth of the next treasure He shared with me. I now could see the treasure of restoration. Psalms 23:3 says, "He restores my soul." I was restored to a relationship with the Father. I had my joy back. I learned to trust and find peace in the Heavenly Father. I was growing in knowledge and wisdom while finding the strength to plunge forward for Christ. I was willing to accept His guidance and let Him direct my life. I had accepted that my Father could do a much better job with my life than I was capable of doing. He was grafting me into a healthier vine so I could bear fruit. From the vine I could get my nourishment and grow. He was positioning me so I could see His purpose in my existence.

I thought about a period of time when I had drifted away from my father and tried to face life on my own. He allowed it while deeply hurting inside. I know he felt rejected, but he never showed it when we were together. He still treasured every moment I spent with him even though there weren't many. He allowed me the time it took to find my way back to the closeness we once had. Once I realized the distance between us was growing, I had to stop. I had to restore our relationship and find my way back to the closeness I once knew. I treated the Heavenly Father the same way. I drifted away; I hurt and rejected Him while He still treasured every little bit of time I spent with Him until I was willing to come to Him for restoration.

After I restored the relationship with my father, transformation started taking place. Quickly I found time had not made a difference. Dad never liked the distance I put between us and just allowed it to be my choice when the gap was closed. He still loved me, spoke to me, spent time with me, tried to guide me, and was there for me any time I was willing to go to him. He never rejected me nor turned his back on me. His love was unconditional. He waited until I wanted the transformation to take place in our relationship and never tried to force it on me.

Transformation with the Heavenly Father was exactly like what I had experienced with my father. He still loved me unconditionally, tried to guide me, wanted my attention, and was there if I would go to Him. He never liked the distance between us, but left the choice of closing the gap up to me. I wanted to be transformed—transformed into the likeness of Him. Transformation is a priceless treasure. My mind and body were being transformed just as the Bible teaches. Romans 12:2 says, "Do not conform any longer to the pattern of this world, be transformed by the renewing of you mind. Then you will be able to test and approve what God's will is—his good, pleasing and perfect will." 2 Corinthians 3:18 says, "And we, who with unveiled faces all reflecting the Lord's glory, are being transformed into his likeness with ever-increasing glory, which comes from the Lord who is the Spirit."

This is what I saw taking place in my life and what the Father wants to take place in everyone's life. My mind was renewed and was focusing on Jesus Christ. Things of the world no longer seemed to matter. I had to stay focused on Jesus and allow Him to be my light. I had to reflect on the glory of God and let Him start to change my entire appearance so it reflected the life of Jesus Himself. Then—and only then—could I see the fruit produced from what I was experiencing? I wanted to see it! I wanted to experience it! I wanted the anointing of the Holy Spirit so I could take my position in the body of Christ.

I had known about all of these treasures and had experienced them to some degree in the past, but this time it was different. The meaning of each treasure had a new definition, and the treasures now had much greater value. They were treasures I had always taken for granted; now they were real jewels and gems deeply rooted into my soul. They were priceless and irreplaceable treasures which could never be lost—only stolen by Satan or regarded as cheap and thrown away by my own choice. Watch out—Satan comes as a thief in the night to kill, steal, and destroy you. You have a choice. Will you accept these treasures? If you accepted them in the past, did you throw them away? Did you let Satan rob you of them? If so, get them back.

Study Questions

Do you fully trust your Heavenly Father?

Do you trust in God's provision for all your needs?

When you feel you have no one to turn to, do you turn to God, whom you can trust?

Do you have peace in your heart? Are you at peace with God?

Do you accept or reject your Father's guidance?

Do you desire more knowledge of God? If so, are you doing anything about it?

Are you gaining strength from the Lord as you daily walk with Him? In what ways are you gaining strength?

Do you form an opinion of God before knowing who He really is?

How strong are you at making the right decisions and sticking by them?

Do you strive to look like Jesus to the world around you?

Are you obedient to God?

Do you love others as much or more than you love yourself?

Do you see any fruit produced in your life?

10

The Narrow Path

Was cherishing the treasures enough? The question coming to mind is whether I am willing to take my relationship with my Father to an even deeper level. Am I willing to allow Him to mold insignificant little me into something significant for Him? If I cherished the treasures, I would want to enjoy them. I kept seeking God and allowing Him to continue to move in mysterious ways in my life. I knew the Heavenly Father loved me and wanted to complete a great work in my life. This was only the beginning, and I knew it. "Being confident of this, that he who began a good work in you will carry it on to completion until the day of Christ Jesus" (Phil. 1:6, NIV). God had started a work in my life, and if I allowed it, He would continue to work in my life until it was completed. Completion would be when I would sit at the feet of the Father Himself in heaven.

So the journey continued. My Father was showing me He desired more from me than I have ever given Him before. He knows the perfect plan for me that would bring glory to His name, and He wants to lead me down the narrow path, guiding me every step of the way. I could really relate to the old-time fairy tale, *The Wonderful Wizard of Oz*. I am sure most of you reading my story have heard the fairy tale at some time in your life. Here is where it all began.

I lived in Hickory, North Carolina, with my husband Jerry, a military man, living a rather comfortable life. I had my real estate business in which I was blessed. I lived in a nice house with far more than I could possibly need. I could look out the windows and see the fabulous view of the lake and watch the sunrise across the water any morning that I wanted. I had a swimming pool in my backyard to enjoy with family and friends, a lushly landscaped lawn with a variety of flowers blooming every season, garden areas enhanced with a koi pond, and large trees to provide shade on a hot summer day. We enjoyed many cookouts on our large back deck and Friday nights sitting in the screen porch fellowshipping with friends and family.

I was happy by all means with a great husband, a successful career, two beautiful grown daughters and three lovely grandchildren. Day-to-day life seemed to go rather smoothly except for the normal disruptions families experience along the way. My grandchildren were at the ages they always made me laugh. My oldest granddaughter was a dainty little girl with silky straight blonde hair and big blue eyes that would twinkle and catch the attention of anyone in the room. She would do the funniest things always bringing back to mind memories of raising her mother. Of course she captured my heart from the very beginning in a special way since she was my first grandchild. I would always say, "She taught me how to be a grandmother," and what a blessing and joy it was. Then there were the fifteen-month-old twins, a boy and a girl. I used to call them my twinkies. If you have ever had a package of Twinkies, you know they are delightful little cakes that come in a package of two with the sweetest filling in the middle. These delightful twins came in a package of two, and they were such a sweet addition to the family. With two babies at once, I was on my toes at all times when they were around. Thank goodness one was a girl! She was born with the natural mothering skills and always tried to teach her brother to do things her way. If she was thirsty, she had to have two cups of juice because her brother had to be thirsty as well. If she was hungry, it was time for both of them to have a snack. My youngest daughter was completing her counseling degree in college. You can see life seemed grand in many ways, and I did not have much to complain about.

Today it was different. I received a call my father had been diagnosed with cancer. It was a cancer very rarely discovered in the early stages, and no cure had been discovered for it yet. My heart skipped a beat at the word *mesothelioma*, and the tears started pouring down my cheeks. A storm was coming. There was a sharp feeling in my gut like a knife had cut right through me. The words penetrated into my mind, the speed of the wind kept picking up, and I was carried miles and miles away thinking about the news and what the outcome could be. The thoughts whirled around in my head like a cyclone hour upon hour that afternoon. Finally, evening set in. Exhausted from crying and thinking, I later crashed into bed, lay down on my pillow, and cried myself to sleep.

The next day I woke up early—still in shock over the sudden news. The sun was shining in my bedroom window, and I knew it was time to face another day. No, I was not in the land of the Munchkins and thanked for killing the Wicked Witch of the East. Here I was, Daddy's little girl right in Hickory, North Carolina, still facing the outcome of the storm that had just hit and had sent me into a new land. My dad was a pastor, a man of God who shared Jesus with many people, and he lived miles and miles away from me. How would I ever get to spend enough time with him and be there for him and my mother the way I would like? Oh, how I wished I could go home!

While Dorothy's house came to rest on the wicked witch and killed her in the fairy tale, I could in no way kill the wicked Satan who deceived Adam and Eve in the first place and caused us to live in a world with sickness along with many other bad things. The difference is Satan is in the north, south, east, and west, seeking all those whom he can devour. Thank goodness we have the Heavenly Father in all four corners of the earth as well to bring the good in our land.

Dorothy was anxious to get back home to her Aunt Em and Uncle Henry. During this storm I was anxious to find my way back into a closer relationship with the King. Dorothy had met other friends (the Munchkins), but they were not the same as being at home with her aunt and uncle. I thought about my friends I had met over the years. It was nice to have friends and fun to do things with them. But definitely they could not fill the void of the Heavenly Father. I was being directed to start a journey down the straight narrow path if I wanted to find the King. It too would lead me to a city far more beautiful than the City of Emeralds. The heavenly city will have walls adorned with every kind of precious stone. The city streets will be pure gold like clear glass, gates of solid pearl, and the glory of God will illumine it, and its lamp will be the Lamb of God. What a beautiful city awaits those who believe in Jesus Christ. We do not need a silly old witch to kiss us on the forehead; we can have the touch of Jesus all over us from head to toe. There is no way to get there but to walk with Jesus and follow the narrow path. No one can take you to this city. No car can drive you there, and no airplane can fly you there. You simply have to get there on your own by your own choice. A quick whirl on Dorothy's heels, and the witch was gone. But it does not matter how many times you turn on your heels and run from God, He always remains with you. "Having shod your feet with the preparation of the gospel of peace" (Eph. 6:15, NASB). My feet are fitted with properly fitted shoes that will never wear out, so I started my journey.

As I journeyed along the path, I saw many houses of various sizes and shapes with people living in them. I stopped to visit with a few friendly people and day after day kept moving on. I know the only way to get to the King is to keep going and bravely resolve not to ever turn back. I had not gone far before realizing I needed to reprogram my brain. I was not like the scarecrow who did not have a brain, but I needed more knowledge and wisdom programmed into my brain. I did not need my head stuffed with things of this world; I needed it filled with wisdom and knowledge only the King could give. So journey on I did and will continue to do until I get to the King who will take me home. I will be like the scarecrow and fall into many holes in the road but try to quickly get back on my feet again and merrily laugh along the way. As the road gets rougher, I will need to apply more diligence, but nevertheless I must keep walking so I can get to the King.

More knowledge and wisdom may change the shape of my head, but it will only be shaped more like the mind of Jesus Christ. Unlike the scarecrow, I do not have to worry if I open my mouth that everything will come out of my head and its shape will change. I was learning along my journey to open my mouth and let all I knew about Jesus Christ come out of my mouth, knowing it may change the shape of someone else. Shaping people for the King is important because it would get them one step closer to home. And "there is no place like our heavenly home."

I thought back to the time before the King opened my ears to hear what was going on, opened my eyes so I could look at Him with a great deal of curiosity. This was my first glimpse of the Kingdom of God. Then He gave me a new nose and mouth. My new nose helped me smell the aroma of the Holy Spirit when He was in the room, and my mouth helped me to open up and share Him with others. The scarecrow walked about in a clumsy manner, and for many years I had walked around in a clumsy manner as well. If only I had a brain programmed to the mind of Christ, the King would not think I was so clumsy.

I was always offered all I wanted spiritually, but I never opened up to take in the nourishment. I felt saddened, for it proved I was not such a good Christian after all. I wasted a lot of time keeping Jesus to myself, not helping the poor and needy like I should, avoiding getting involved in ministry, and spending very little time digging into the Word of God. If only I had, the evil one would not have swooped in and deceived me in so many ways.

After I managed to reprogram my brain, my journey continued down the narrow path. Next, I found myself quite rusty. I had stayed in the same position for quite some time and never grew in my walk with the Lord. Remember, I had become a good benchwarmer and went through the motions without any fruit or growth in our Father-daughter relationship. I needed to get the oil can off the shelf and oil my joints until I was free from rust if I was going to pursue a new heart. I needed a transformed heart, a refreshed heart in Christ Jesus. I wanted to put my treasure in Jesus so my heart would be there as well. I needed to journey on so I could get a heart filled with more compassion and love for others—one that when I see my sister or brother in need would be willing to share my world's goods and blessings with them.

I needed to make sure my heart was free from bitter jealousy and selfish ambition. I knew a heart conditioned for Jesus was much more valuable than anything else I could ask for. If I had a renewed brain full of knowledge and a happy heart, I was making progress down the narrow path. While I was not made of shiny tin, I did want my body to shine brightly for the Son of God. I did not want to meet with the King at the end of the path and tell Him I had not been obedient to His commands. I would not want Him to think I had remained rusty all my life. I decided to take the oilcan—the Word of God—with me so whenever I started to get rusty, I could loosen up and keeping searching for a heart like His.

Following the narrow path, I went deep into the wilderness. I had been journeying along the well-marked path, but the woods became very thick and dark. There were times I just wanted to get out of the wilderness and step out in the open country and see the sunshine. In the wilderness there was always something prowling about, but I knew once I was out of the wilderness, I would once again dwell in a beautiful land and have nothing to fear. I was following the Holy Spirit, yet at times I still felt like a coward. It was a mystery to me, but I suppose I was born that way. Others think I am always brave, but many times I turn into a coward, afraid of what the Holy Spirit is directing me or asking me to do. I know this is not right, and I just need to fully trust the Spirit to guide me in all truth like He promised He would do. I was very grateful my brain was being reprogrammed. My heart was being transformed. Now all I needed was boldness to do what the Spirit was leading me to do and not be a coward. I must continue my journey to meet the King and not lose sight of what I am after. Once I see the King, I will have found my way home and I always must remember "there is no place like my heavenly home."

Many nights in the wilderness I could not sleep. I was lonely without my dad. I was hungry for the Word of God and the comfort He would give me. I kept looking for the springs of living water to quench my thirst.

I had to fight my way through this wilderness and not lose sight of where I was headed or what I was searching for. I had found my joy and peace; I continued on and learned to tune into the voice of God, stumbled on a new measure of faith, went to the river for a cleansing, deeply rooted my branch into the true vine so I could bear fruit, already discovered a treasure chest full of treasures, started building an intimate relationship with the Father, and caught sight of this deteriorating building being restored and prepared for ministry, so what did I have to be afraid of? I had no reason to be a coward, for my Father promised to equip me for whatever He would call me to do. I had no choice but to continue to journey on toward the King. The King would never challenge or require me to do things I was not equipped to do.

I was terribly afraid of falling off the course of life God had planned for me, but there was nothing to do but try it. I will simply need to learn how to pick myself back up when I do fail and try one more time. Because being afraid to attempt to do my part of the kingdom work was not the way it was supposed to be, I had to put forth effort and try. Little by little I could see progress in accomplishing the tasks I was called to do. Training and equipping took place first, and then the task became easier to accomplish. If I could only remember I am marked and sealed as a child of the King, I would know I can call on Him for protection at any time. I felt like the beast would surely tear me apart, but I know I will fight them as long as I am alive.

I drew a long breath of relief knowing I would live a little while longer, and I am glad for it will be my opportunity to show God how much I love Him and want to please Him by doing my part in the body of Christ. When the creatures frighten me, I know my heart will skip a beat, but I will continue on. I could not lose sight of where I was going. I had to fight my way through the wilderness. I had to stay focused on the trail and continue the search.

One morning I woke up knowing I had to push on through the wilderness and get across the river the path ran through. I stood on the bank of the river at the end of the trail and could see it pick back up on the other side. Somehow I would get across. At times the current was swift, and it tried to drag me downstream further and further away from my Heavenly Father. The water grew so deep I felt like I could not touch the bottom, but I could not allow Satan to carry me into a foreign land. I had to avoid letting Satan enchant me and make me his slave. I was getting my brain reprogrammed and my heart transformed, and my courage was increasing. Now when the people around me are stuck in the deep waters, I will be willing to try and rescue them.

When I feel like I have gone off course, I must follow the Holy Spirit until I am back on the road once again walking toward the King. I must pick up my life where I left off and get back on the path from which I was carried away. I will need to walk as fast as I can and stop to help everyone I meet along the way. I must be ready to step out in the water and rescue anyone I see drowning. I cannot let the least of my friends drown in the lies and deceit of Satan. I will call on the King for help, and He will tell me what to do since He is in the business of rescuing people.

As I walk along the path of life, I want to take time to listen to the singing of the birds and look at the lovely flowers. I want to enjoy all their colors and the brightness they add to the countryside. I want to slow down long enough to enjoy the scent of the flowers and just breathe in their aroma until I fall asleep each evening, knowing it is a glorious gift from God. If I see a friend trapped in the deadly flowers surrounding them, I want to come beside that friend and carry them through the deadly flower fields and lead them into the grassy green fields where they can find courage to grow in Christ Jesus and listen to the voice of the Holy Spirit.

I want to do my part to free people from the enemy and bring them into the glorious presence of the Living God. I want to see them coming up to Jesus and say in a soft squeaky voice, "Thank you for saving my life." I hope to see them bow down to the King and cry out to Him in a shrill voice, acknowledging Him as the Prince of Peace. I hope to see people scampering in all directions to do work for the Kingdom and chasing after the lost to share Jesus with them. I hope to hear people ask, "Is there anything I can do to repay Jesus for the life He gave up for me?" and the reply will simply be, "Oh, yes, you can disciple others and rescue your friends." There are thousands of people who need to come to Jesus, and we need to go and get them at once. Hopefully we will see them run in all directions as fast as possible to come to the foot of the cross and meet Jesus. We need to be working so fast because time is limited. The results could be astounding if we all get to work. Your friends may be drowning in the river of addiction to alcohol or drugs. They may be caught up in a life of lies, stealing, or deceit. They may be absorbed in a life of sexual immorality or one of many other things destroying them and keeping them from a relationship with the Father. The weight of their burden may be so big and heavy you think you could not possibly be used to rescue them. But I know the King will be pleased if you bring them to Him, and He will thank you ever so much.

People need to be coming from all directions—thousands of them at a time, from every tribe and nation, just to meet the King of Kings. Our hearts should desire to lead everyone we meet that does not know Jesus out of the poisonous scent of Satan and into the loving arms of Jesus. Every time they need us we should hear them call us again and we should come to their assistance.

In my journey through the wilderness I once again meditated on the death of Jesus—the painful, humiliating death when He was beaten and hung on the cross in front of all those people. I was humbled knowing He did all this to save my life. So hereafter I must serve Him and obey His every wish and command. I knew I could no longer scamper in all directions but instead had to stay on the path. I would continually ask the question, "What else can I do to repay You for saving my life?"

The King will let everyone who is willing to come into His presence to come. He sits day after day in the great throne room of heaven, and even though I cannot see His face, I will wait upon Him. It is hard to tell what He may look like in person, but I do know He is loving and kind. He is full of mercy and grace, and He has to be amazing if He could speak the world into existence in just six days. He would continue to reprogram my brain, transform my heart, and increase my courage. It does not matter how far I travel down the path, He would never ever send me back where I came from. He was preparing a place for me where I will never have to be hungry, I will never be sick, I will never be sad, and I would always be in the arms of the One who loves me.

Just the excitement and the promise of it all helps keep my focus on walking down the narrow path to get to the King. One day I know I will get there, and the big gate will swing open. All the saints will pass through and find themselves in the throne room with the King. Everything will be glistening with countless emeralds, gold, glass, pearls, and more. The King will be seated on His throne, and those who are worthy will approach Him with reverence and awe. It is so hard to imagine what it will be like when I get to see the King, and praise and worship is all I will do. When I get to enter His presence and I am surrounded by His glory, what will my heart feel like? I cannot wait to bow down and thank the King for bringing me home.

I am sure the Heavenly City will sparkle with the beautiful streets of gold. There will be many men, women, and children walking around in the brilliant glory of the Lord because they decided to follow Jesus. The King will be delighted if we make ourselves at home once He brings us into His presence, yet I know I will feel small and meek. Although I bear the mark on my forehead, I know I will still humble myself before the King because He is strong and I am weak. I will be so delighted to see Him that I think I will just fall at His feet. He will not ask me to do anything else to stay in my heavenly home. He has made room for me and plans to keep me with Him for all eternity.

Since I was asking now for a new brain, a changed heart, and an increase in courage, He was already granting my request. The King is not the great and terrible; He is merely the Great King. He loves you and me so much He will give us what we ask for here and now. The King's desire is for us to look like a child of the King, so He will not withhold His characteristics from us.

The journey was teaching me to avoid the wicked, fierce Satan. Although he will sneak up and get me at times, I was learning to be on guard. I know he has a whole group of evil helpers, and they come running from all directions like a pack of great wolves with fierce eyes and sharp teeth. He will do his best to try and make me a slave to him, but I will fight him and tell him to get behind me. Every time Satan sees I have defeated him, I know he will become even angrier and send another monkey my way to try to devour me, so I need to stay alert. Satan's only wish is that I fail at serving the King. I could only wish one day the evil one would see the mark on my forehead and leave me alone. I wish he would stop trying to harm me and carry me away. I often tell him he is a wicked creature and excitedly wait for the day he is thrown into the abyss and can no longer harm anyone nor lead anyone astray. Thank goodness I will not be given the task of killing Satan. The King will take care of Satan Himself.

When this happens, there will be great rejoicing among the children of God. We had been deceived many times during the years, and Satan will be defeated in the end. We will be united together and go home at last. At times I drifted off the path and lost my way, but I know where the Heavenly City is, and I am continuing to journey in that direction. It may be a long way off; it may be merely years or months away, or it may tomorrow or at the very next breath I breathe. But when the time comes, I will not need any monkey to catch me up in their arms and fly me away. Instead, "the Lord Himself will descend from heaven with a shout, with the voice of the archangel and with the trumpet of God, and the dead in Christ will rise first. Then we who are alive and remain will be caught up with them in the clouds to meet the Lord in the air, and so shall we always be with the Lord" (1 Thess. 4:16–17, NASB).

The enemy will be defeated, and the King of kings, who is everywhere but to the eyes of common mortals is not visible, will be seated on the throne, and I will finally be able to converse with Him. I will go and claim the promise He made to me and to all other believers, He will prove Himself to be faithful and true, and the promise will be fulfilled.

Although each one of us may see God in a different way, we will not be fooled. It will be no mistake that we are allowed to enter into the throne room. It is no trick; God is not trying to amuse us and keep us busy. He is not trying to order us around; instead, He gives us a free choice. He is not coloring our world completely green because He knows everything is not always beautiful.

There is no magic or mystical way to get home. It is simply accepting Jesus as your companion and following the narrow path. Christian life does not always agree with us, but it is important to show others how much you have grown in Christ Jesus. Walking down the path with Jesus toward the King should come with ease if we really love Him. The trees in the wilderness may grow thick at times. The days may seem dark and dreary. You may experience pain along the way, but you can pass safely through it and come out victorious one day. I will still bump into many high walls. Sometimes I will fall off, and other times I will climb over them and find something better on the other side. If I fall off the wall, I will always end up in pain and need to go through the restoration process. In the end, I know the King will look up and say, "My darling child, you are home." I hope I can cover His face with kisses and show Him how glad I am to be home.

Although I will come out of the wilderness, I know the road will not end until I go be with the Lord in Heaven. Until then, I will journey down the road every day, expecting surprises and obstacles along the way. God's desire was for me to accept the gifts He would present to me along the way. He would not want me to get frustrated and run the other direction or feel overwhelmed. The journey may take me out of my comfort zone and point me in an entirely different direction, but following the road will get me to my final destination—my home in heaven with my Father.

Study Questions

Has your life been interrupted lately? Do you feel like you are in the midst of a storm?

Do you truly believe God is with you as you go through your storm? If not, what keeps you from feeling His presence and knowing He is right with you?

Do you have goals in life that may be different from the goals God has for you? If so, are you willing to put them aside and follow after God's plans for you?

Do you feel insignificant in the Kingdom of God? What do you think it will take to make you feel significant?

Do you look at the things God is asking you to do in a positive way? Do you desire to please Him and step out in faith believing you can accomplish them with His help?

Is your heart fully yielded to serving Him, or could you use a transformed heart? In what ways do you need your heart to be transformed? What do you think is missing in your heart?

Is your brain programmed with knowledge and wisdom from the Word of God? Do you need to invest more time in learning about the nature of Jesus and how to walk in a manner pleasing to God?

Are you equipped with courage enough to step out in faith believing and knowing you can do all things through Christ in whom your strength is found? If not, what steps can you take to increase your courage and trust in God so that whatever He asks of you, you can do?

Are you on the path that leads toward home? Are you excited about going home and being with the King for all eternity?

11

Truths Revealed

The Heavenly Father wanted me to experience a life fully dependent on Him, fully devoted to Him, fully obedient to Him, and fully trusting in Him. I had to remain aware that all distractions and obstacles would be Satan interfering. At these times I would hang on to the Apostle Paul's encouragement in 2 Corinthians 12:10: "Therefore, I am well content with weakness, with insults, with distresses, with persecutions, with difficulties, for Christ's sake; for when I am weak, then I am strong." Yes, we may be weak in our natural selves, but we have strength in Christ. Paul goes on to say in Romans 6:22, "But now having been freed from sin and enslaved to God, you derive your benefit, resulting in sanctification, and the outcome, eternal life." I am set free on the road toward heaven so my journey goes on. The end result will be sanctification and eternal life with the Father. Until that time, I will continue to seek His face and build a closer, more intimate relationship with the Father.

An intimate relationship is what God wants first and foremost from every Christian. If we have this intimate relationship, we can clearly understand what He wants from us. His will for all believers is that we look like Jesus, act like Jesus, and share Jesus with others. "The one who says he abides in Him ought himself to walk in the same manner as He walked" (1 John 2:6, NASB). If you claim to have Jesus in your heart, walk like Jesus walked. Let our life reflect Jesus to others and look like a child of God. You will be doing the will of God as long as your hearts are right with Him and you are obeying His commands.

Reaching out and feeling the hand of God walking beside me, I merely continue to cry out for more and more. I want Him to teach me and equip me to better serve Him. I know He has greater plans for me, and I want to find out what the plans are. In my prayers I started asking God to allow me to know some of the mysteries about Him. I petitioned Him to continue dreaming with me and feed my mind in my sleep. I asked Him to minister to me and teach me to minister to others. I want as much spiritual food as I can get. I was always hungry for more food, and He was setting a banquet before me to indulge in.

So indulge I did. I started searching for food. I was studying the Bible every chance I got and spending hours in prayer. I read book after book on seeking God and various topics on the Holy Spirit. I continued praying for wisdom, understanding, and discernment. I wanted to be careful as I read the Bible and allow the Holy Spirit to direct me in all truth. I started to understand the Bible for myself, not just hang on to all the things I was taught. I wanted to learn from others, but I realized I had been stuck believing so many things I merely heard rather than searching out the truth for myself. You can easily be deceived when you put your trust in man. I believed many things based on religion and tradition rather than on understanding the Word of God. There are so many different interpretations and translations of the Bible. I just wanted to understand it the way the Holy Spirit wanted me to understand it. I wanted to only pull truth from reading and studying myself and not be influenced by opinions. I was starving for facts about my Father. The facts would show me who He really was instead of just who I had been told He was. I wanted to know Him from personal experience, just like I did my dad. I know many people trace back their genealogy to find out any and every detail of their family and often make a book out of the information they gather. So I was on a mission to gather information. I may not write it in a book, but I just needed to know the details for myself.

As I gathered the information, I felt like I was a little girl sitting on His lap, absorbing intimate time with Him. The Heavenly Father connects with His children just like I had a father-and-daughter connection with my dad. If you want to experience this type of connection with God, you must open your mind, allowing the Holy Spirit to teach you. You have to recognize His voice so you can be taught, and you must be willing to change your thinking where necessary. You have to let God out of the box you have kept Him contained in. When someone gives you a present, you are ready to open it as soon as possible to see what is inside. It may have a big pretty bow that you can't wait to rip off and get to the gift inside, but I wonder why it is so easy to just leave God sealed in the box. I guess we think the tape will hold Him in the box and we can keep Him to ourselves, but—trust me—He knows how to get out on His own even if we choose to contain Him. So why not let Him out on your own? If you do, it will be an even greater gift—one you will enjoy and treasure.

Knowing my dad came naturally since I heard his audible voice, saw him almost every day of my life, grew up in the same house he lived in, and since his blood was my blood. I could look at pictures of my dad and see what he looked like as a toddler, young boy, teenager, and young adult. There was no question what my father looked like. I could pick him out of any crowd. My Father God wanted to live in the same house and wanted me to see Him every day—and His blood is my blood since I am His child. While there may not be a physical portrait of God, you can get a picture of the Heavenly Father by looking at His Son, Jesus. I was fortunate to have a father with many characteristics of Jesus. Every father needs to give his children a picture of what the Heavenly Father looks like so they can recognize His appearance in any crowd. Children need a father who says, "This is my beloved son/daughter." They need to feel unconditional love, acceptance, comfort, and protection from their father. Children need to be able to experience the treasures in their father that are found in the Heavenly Father. It will aid children in understanding the great love the Heavenly Father wants to lavish on them. We can all lose our dads like I had experienced, but we all have an undying Father. You will never be left alone in this world.

Easter Sunday was approaching. I thought about the depth of love the Heavenly Father has for each one of us. Imagine if you were asked to give up your one and only son as a sacrifice. Imagine giving up a son without blemish or defect whom you loved from the depths of your heart. Could you do it? Could you give him up just to show others how much you were willing to sacrifice for them? I don't think many (if any) of us would. Yet our Heavenly Father loves us so much He sent His only begotten Son, who was faced with everything on earth. He was sent as a human just like us to experience trials and tribulations and set an example for us to follow. Being saved as a child and giving my heart to Jesus had been a mere start years ago. I had to give *all* my heart, *all* my talents, *all* my resources, *all* my soul, and *all* my life if necessary—all for the cause of Christ. Nothing can be allowed to stand in the way. If I knew Jesus—really knew Him—I would know my Father. You too can enter into a relationship with Jesus and get to know your Heavenly Father. He wants you to give Him all you have. Because Jesus lives, we can face every day living in victory. Look on the cross where Jesus died and picture the sacrifice made for you. It is time to make sacrifices for Him. It was a much greater example of the sacrifice my father had made in order to provide all my needs and many of my desires while I was growing up. I know my father would have laid his life down for me. What pleasure it would be if I had the opportunity to tell my dad one more time how much I love him. I do have the pleasure of showing and telling the Heavenly Father continually how much I love Him. My dad had to say good-bye, and he told me he was going home to be with the Lord. But I thank God I never have to say goodbye to Him because I will spend eternity with my Father.

Study Questions

Can you tell when God is trying to change the direction of your life?

Does the change feel more like a distraction in your life? Do you find yourself frustrated or annoyed when God changes the course of your life?

Do you accept the change or rebel and question God?

Are you craving more of the Jesus in your life, or are you sitting back content feeling you have enough?

Matthew 5:6 says, "Blessed are those who hunger and thirst for righteousness, for they shall be satisfied." Do you hunger and thirst for righteousness?

Are you confident the God who began a good work in you will carry on until it is completed?

Are you willing to invest time in getting to know your Father? If so, list ways you will accomplish getting to know Him better.

12

"Do You Love Me?"

Knowing how Jesus sacrificed for me, I committed to being a living sacrifice for Him. I knew once I made this commitment, I would be put to the test. I was at a point in my life where all I felt I needed was my Father, and nothing else I had or wanted even mattered any longer. When I returned to work after my father's death, I tried to keep busy to take my mind off of the loss. Now I was focusing my mind on the Father and knew I needed to get busy.

I fell asleep praying one evening, and within a couple of hours, I woke up from a dream. I remembered the dream, and in it the Lord was asking me if I was willing to sell everything I have and take up the cross and follow Him. Was this what my commitment to sacrifice was going to include? In the dream, Jesus asked me three times—just like He did Peter when he asked him if he loved Him. The first time I was asked, I responded yes. Then in the dream I was told that it was Jesus who was asking the question, and He knew I didn't mean it. I was then told to get serious and answer the question once again. Again I replied yes. The voice said, "This is Jesus you are dealing with, and I even know your mind and your thoughts, so you can't fool Me." For the third time I was asked the question: "Are you willing to sell everything, take up the cross, and follow Me?" This time I was broken with tears streaming down my face, and I said, "Yes, Lord, I am willing."

Then in the dream I was shown my house sitting on the lake and a flash of all my possessions within the home and told I was to sell it.

Bargaining with Jesus, I told Him if He wanted the house sold, He would just have to send someone to my front door wanting the house and everything in it. I told Him I did not want to go through marketing the house, so if it was really what He wanted done, He would just have to do it. Jesus responded, "Okay, don't forget I can do anything I want to do; this is Jesus you are bargaining with." Jesus told me so few were willing to give up everything it required to be a disciple for Him, and He needed more. He was looking for obedient people no matter what the cost.

Once out of the daze I was in from being sound asleep and dreaming, I lay there in bed thinking about how Jesus approached the twelve disciples. He asked them to leave everything behind and take up the cross and follow Him. He asked if they were willing to do so. It is easy to think you would give everything up. You hear of others selling everything to move to another country somewhere as a missionary, but it is a completely different feeling when you are hit with this question directly. You must never say yes if you don't mean it. I fell back asleep hours later, knowing I needed to question my willingness to answer this question with a true heartfelt yes.

In the morning when the alarm went off, the question popped back into my mind immediately and remained there the entire day. Was it just a dream, or was it something God really wanted me to do? Was He really asking me to sell my home, give up all I had, take up the cross, and follow Him? Just what did He mean by *all*? Was it all possessions, all self, or possibly both? Did He want me to just rid my mind of all thoughts of earthly things? Where would He want me to go? Deep down, I felt like the Lord was asking me to really give up my home and all the stuff I had accumulated. God was looking for me without any distractions. He was looking for my full attention.

It was easy to think I was willing, but if the true test came, could I trust God enough to just sell everything I had, not knowing where or what I was to do next? Could I be like James and John, get out of my comfortable boat, and simply drop everything to go anywhere and do anything and everything He wanted? It may seem like an easy question to answer, but it wasn't. I did not want to answer halfheartedly. I wanted to say yes and mean it from the bottom of my heart. I wanted to say yes in reality, not just in a dream. My husband and I had just completed construction of our dream home on the lake, and every room was beautifully decorated. Our boat sat on the dock, ready to ride down the river at any moment. My mother had an apartment in our basement, and selling our house would mean taking her home as well. Would I be willing if this was what He really wanted? Jesus was everything to me, and today I pictured Him as the Lamb of God—gentle, meek, humble, soft, and patient, just like the Father sent Him. He was being patient with me as I was being molded for whatever He had in store for me. I fell in bed exhausted by the end of the day, pondering this question that was consuming my mind. I was just absorbed by the presence of the Lord.

For the next two days, I could not get the question out of my mind. It was beginning to make me feel tired and worn out. I think I was trying to sort out if it really would happen and what the next step for Jesus would be. My brain was racing ahead, and I simply needed to answer the direct question. I went to work, returned home, and went straight to bed after dinner the first day. On the second evening, I took the opportunity to share with my husband the dream. I knew if this was to really happen, he would have to be willing as well. By the look on his face, I was certain he hoped it was just a dream. Coming out of the military, he was tired of moving. He was ready to be settled for the rest of his life in this house. It was the perfect setting for a retired person. Beautiful sunrises in the morning and sunsets in the evening on the lake, fishing from the dock, and a quick trip down the river at any time—what more could he ask for? Maybe I was just being tested to see if I would pick up my fear, say no, and run from God or hang on to my selfish desires. Maybe God had a plan for me that I was not aware of yet, or maybe God just wanted to see if I was willing. Whatever the case, I knew God was waiting for an answer.

On the third day, I was ready with my answer. "Heavenly Father, I am willing to give up everything I have and take up the cross and follow You.

I desire to have You lead and direct my life." I did not want anything to stand in the way of my relationship with Him. I thought back to when my father was dying with cancer, and I knew I would have willingly given up anything if it would keep him alive. How much more the Heavenly Father deserves. Why shouldn't I be willing to give up everything to keep Him alive?

Once I said yes, I just went about my day-to-day life. Nothing happened over the next few months, so I resolved in myself it must have been a dream to see if I was willing. The dream came to my mind at the most unusual times, and I kept reminding myself I would not let worldly possessions stand in the way of my relationship with my Father that I had been working so hard to build. Months turned into a year, and then I was approaching the end of the second year. The dream never went away, and I started sharing the dream with some of my friends and telling them, "I believe it will really happen."

The day came when the dream would become a reality. While talking to a friend of mine in the real estate business, he asked me if I had any interest in selling my home. He had some friends interested in buying a vacation home on the lake from Cairo, Egypt. He thought my house would be perfect for them. Their brother and his family had purchased another home in the neighborhood, so being close together would be very convenient. Flashes of the dream jumped into my head, and I wondered if God was really going to bring a buyer right to my front door as I had dreamed. I agreed to let them look at the house to see if they were even interested. Of course no commitment to sell was made at this time, so there was no harm in letting them look, and there was a possibility they may not even like my home.

They arrived the next morning to see the house. The sales agent jumped out in me, and I found myself selling the features in my home. I even spent hours the night before making sure everything was clean and orderly. I gave them the grand tour and walked them back to the foyer to say good-bye. The couple looking at my home began to have a conversation between each other speaking in their native language. Of course I did not understand a word they were saying, and the expressions on their faces did not give anything away so I just stood there listening, wondering, and—you guessed it—remembering the dream.

After completing their conversation together, they popped the question: "Would you talk to your husband and give us a price for the house—completely furnished?" Surely not my comfy king-sized bed, which I had to step on a side stool to climb into. I felt like a princess when I laid my head on my king-sized feather pillow, and I could sleep like a baby. They wanted the decorator items. I thought, *Surely not the ones with special memories attached or the ones I shopped so diligently to find.* They wanted pictures on the walls with the exception of family photographs but said I could leave those as well if I would like. Lamps—no problem; I could always find a lamp. Area rugs—I hoped not my Persian one. Towels hanging in the bathrooms (well some were the fancy decorator kind and they matched my nautical theme so well) and even the sheets and bedspreads on the beds were part of it. You want bed linens? Okay, I could replace them with the same colors and new ones. They wanted to buy the house like it was with everything in it.

Imagine that! Someone coming to my door, looking at my house (which I never advertised), and asking me for the price I would take for my home. Either this was God, or I was having another dream. I said I was willing to sell. God sent the buyer to me—just like He said He would do—and they wanted everything. After a lengthy family discussion and much prayer, we set a price at which we would be willing to sell. My husband was not as eager, but he would never hold me back from being obedient to my Father. He knew deep inside if the dream came to reality, it must be God.

Two days later I called and gave our price. They thought it over for a few brief moments and called back saying yes. Several things occurred along the way causing a slight delay, but all along I knew the dream would be fulfilled, even to the very last detail. Six months later all the details were worked out, and the contract was signed. We moved three weeks later, leaving house and furnishings behind. The dream was something my Father really wanted me to do. Not knowing where the journey would take us, we willingly obeyed what God was asking at the time.

I immediately started praying, "Lord, where do You want me to go, and what shall I spend on a home?" The same night I prayed this prayer, I awoke with instructions in my mind that seemed kind of odd. I sensed I was to spend one half of the money and put the other half up for Kingdom work. This was strange to me, for I felt I should not even have a home. If God wanted me to give everything up, why would He still want me to own any home at all? I was ready to rent and wait on the Lord. I sensed God was directing me to a particular home and to the amount I was to offer. But I was so afraid I was moving too fast, and I just needed to be still and know that He was God. I did not want to displease Him in any way if I had gone so far as to sell my home and leave all my worldly possessions behind.

The nagging thought did not go away. I kept thinking of this home and the amount to offer in my mind, knowing as a realtor it would be insulting to any seller. How on earth could I do this? It was well below the appraised value placed on the home. It was a new home with many lovely features, so I kept questioning why…While this did not make any sense at all, God, of course, was in control.

The next day I decided to go spend some time in the home, and I asked a friend to join me. We spent some time praying in the home together because it was important I knew it was the will of God before I dare have another home. As I prayed, I asked God to give me confirmation if this was where He wanted to place my family. I kept asking myself why God would want me to have this lovely new home if I was asked to sell the one I had. It made no sense at all to me. After some time in prayer, my friend looked up at me and said, "This home feels like you, and I think the Lord wants you to have it. It is really you. God is using you as an example, and His desire is for you to be willing to be obedient to His will. He wants you to have a nice home but just to spend less on a home. He is trying to get your attention to acknowledge He is most important. You can still have a nice home spending half the amount."

I struggled with this for a day and finally decided I would offer the purchase price I had in mind. I shared with the builder of the home what God was doing in my life and simply made the offer. I told him I would understand if he could not do it, but it was all I could offer because the Lord had set the amount I could spend. I felt like he might have wanted to smack me in the face because as a real estate broker I knew better than to insult a seller with a low offer. He merely said, "Let me to talk to my wife, and I will get back with you tomorrow."

I left our appointment feeling like an idiot for sharing my story and making the offer. Had I missed God? Did I just want this nice house for myself? Lord, do I want something nice again to satisfy myself? I prayed as I fell asleep that night asking God to shut the door if it was not His will. I would rather rent a simple apartment until I knew I was in the will of God before I dared to have another nice home.

Early the next morning my phone rang, and I saw it was his phone number. Fear came over me, but I managed to answer his call. After the normal hello and the exchanging of how each was doing for the day, the gentleman merely said, "I talked this over with my wife last night, and we will accept your offer." He explained the financial difficulties they were experiencing, and the amount I offered would pay off the debt and avoid a bank foreclosure on the home. Amidst the shock of the phone call and his response to my offer, I still knew God was in control of this situation, and I would merely move forward in obedience.

Was selling my home just a test to see if I was willing? Was it a test to see if I would sacrifice all I had to please God? Did He think I had invested too much in material possessions rather than in the Kingdom? Was he simply stripping my husband and me from the desire to have stuff we did not need? Was God working on our pride? It may have been only one of these, or it may have been them all. Regardless, He had our attention, and we were growing in our listening and obedience to the Father.

Acknowledging my Father and giving Him the respect He deserved, He continued to transform my mind. I wore a new smile, a natural smile even after giving up my home, and I noticed I had more and more opportunities to be bold for Christ. I was bragging about the Father everywhere I went. It was becoming a natural thing to just bring up the subject of God and what He was doing in my life. I had a deep love for my dad and an even deeper love for the Heavenly Father, and I could not begin to conceive all that He had planned for me. 1 Corinthians 2:9 says, "No eye has seen, no ear has heard, no mind has conceived what God has prepared for those who love Him." He has great things prepared for me on earth and even greater things prepared for me in heaven because I love Him! Decide to love Him and see what He has prepared for you.

In today's world, God needs more disciples. He is in need of an army marching forward into battle for Him. The battle plan is already designed, and He is waiting for enlisted soldiers. He needs soldiers without fear of where they will be sent into battle—soldiers who will wear the full armor of God, knowing it will be their protection. Our Father needs soldiers standing on the frontline, sounding the trumpet loud and clear. He needs soldiers willing to follow directions and stay focused on the target. He needs soldiers willing to lead others into battle with the enemy and walk away victorious. The world is in need of wise soldiers who can separate truth from lies and not be deceived. The army needs strong soldiers who won't buckle under heavy weight when it is tossed upon their backs and strong ones who can carry the load and go the extra mile. The recruiter is making every effort to enlist this army, and we need to accept the signup bonus and go into training. The pay will be greater than any money we can earn, and the retirement package lasts for all eternity. His army needs you today! Don't delay!

Study Questions

If the Holy Spirit spoke to you and asked you to sell everything you had and take up the cross and follow Him, what would your reaction be? Would you be willing to do it?

What does it really mean to take up the cross and follow Him?

Are you willing to get out of the boat and go anywhere God wants to send you? To attempt every task He asks of you?

Are you placing too much value on earthly things? Are you a prideful person of the material possessions you have obtained?

What earthly things distract you from full obedience to God?

Are you signed up to fight in the army for God? To tackle the battles you will come up against?

13

A Father's Love

Once you recognize and accept the depths of the treasures and gifts the Heavenly Father has for you through His Son Jesus Christ, He is looking for how you will return these gifts to Him and how you will share them with others. Can you trust His voice and know when it is Him speaking? Will you obey the voice even if you don't like what is said? Will you allow the Father to discipline you? Will you allow Him to guide every step of your life? Is your faith strong enough to believe you can do all things the Father asks you to do? Can you forgive others as He has forgiven you? Can you restore all your broken relationships? Ask yourself all these questions, and keep asking them over and over again until you can say yes to all of them. When you can answer yes, you are ready to leave the wilderness. So I left the wilderness with a restored life. The next time I enter the wilderness, I want to go there by my own choice. I want to go there like Jesus did—of His own free will, just to be with the Father, and learn from Him.

Trust must be obtained first in order to give any other gift back to God the Father. You take your first step by trusting that God did send His son Jesus to die on the cross for your sins and that this is the only way to the Father. You have to learn to trust Him in all things and believe Father knows best. You have to trust that the Holy Bible is the inspired Word of God and become willing to read it, allowing it to speak to you. You have to trust He will never leave you or forsake you. "No man will be able to stand before you all the days of your life, just as I have been with Moses,

I will be with you; I will not fail you or forsake you" (Josh. 1:5–6, NASB). You have to trust Him with all your heart, not trust Him halfheartedly. "Trust in the Lord with all your heart and do not lean on your own understanding" (Prov. 3:5, NASB). You are required to acknowledge who God is, and He will direct your path. "In all your ways acknowledge Him and He will make your paths straight" (Prov. 3:6, NASB).

Trust is not just a word; it is an action. You must learn to trust God the same way you learn to trust others. You must give Him the benefit of trusting until He proves Himself untrustworthy (and this will never happen). Serving God requires an unwavering and unending trust. A trust that knows that when you jump into His arms, He will catch you. A trust that knows He will provide all your needs. A trust that He will catch you when you fall and pick you up out of the miry clay, setting you back on solid ground. He needs a trust greater than any other trust you give to anyone or anything else. Just like the Father is giving you the gift of someone you can trust, God wants you to return the gift by giving Him someone He can trust in return. Can He trust you to take care of the poor by sharing your blessings? Can He trust you to share Him with others? Can He trust you to cast all your cares on Him? Can He trust you to heal the brokenhearted? Can He trust you to bring freedom to those in bondage? Can He trust you to lay hands on the sick and pray for them? Can He trust you in every way with no conditions attached? I think you get the picture that God deserves someone He can trust.

If you return trust, you will be obedient. Obedience is the next gift you need to give to God. Jesus made obedience simple for you by explaining the two laws that summarize all the laws. In Matthew 22:36–39 Jesus is asked the question, "Teacher, which is the greatest commandment in the Law?' Jesus replied, 'Love the Lord your God with all your heart and with all your soul and with all your mind. This is the first and greatest commandment. And the second is like it: Love your neighbor as yourself.'" You have to open your heart to receive His correction and discipline. You have to listen to His voice and come before Him with full repentance and humbleness, willing to submit to His directions. You must realize He has your best interest at heart, and He knows what rules you need to submit to in order to live a righteous and holy life. He knows what you need to avoid so you do not hurt yourself or others. Our Father knows which rules will bring you joy, peace, comfort, and what will keep you safe. Obedience is important in your Christian walk. The Bible instructs you to obey your father and mother. "Children, obey your parents in the Lord, for this is right" (Eph. 6:1, NASB). Obedience is the way you show the Father you love Him. "If you love me, you will keep my commandments" (John 14:15, NIV). You can and must give the gift of obedience to your Heavenly Father to show Him you accept the gift of guidance He gives you.

If you are willing to be obedient, you will step out in faith. Faith is an extremely important gift the Father needs to see you utilize. Your first step of faith happens when you believe in Jesus Christ, a man we cannot see. It is this faith that sets you free. "Jesus said to the woman, 'your faith has saved you; go in peace'" (Luke 7:50, NASB). "Therefore since we have been justified through faith, we have peace with God through the Lord Jesus Christ, through whom we have gained access by faith into this grace in which we now stand" (Rom. 5:1–2, NIV). Through Jesus Christ it is your faith that gives you access to God the Father.

From this time forward, the gift of faith you give back to God is up to you. With faith, you can do all things through Christ, who gives you strength. If you tap into this strength, the possibilities of what you can accomplish for God are unlimited. "I can do all things through Him who strengthens me" (Phil. 4:13, NASB). With faith you can make a difference in the lives of many people—just like Jesus did. In John 14:12 Jesus says, "Anyone who has faith in me will do what I have been doing. He will do even greater things than these." Are you doing the things that Jesus did—or better yet, doing greater things than He did? With faith you can seek your destiny with God and accomplish it. "Now faith is the assurance of things hoped for, the conviction of things not seen" (Heb. 11:1, NASB). By faith, you can have victory over all sin. "In addition to all, taking up the shield of faith with which you will be able to extinguish all the flaming arrows of the evil one" (Eph. 6:16, NASB). Faith is the gift that keeps on giving. You cannot give it once and think it is enough. This gift you give your Father is priceless to Him. He is pleased when you step out in faith and He sees you using this gift. It is then He can really work through you. It is a gift too large to wrap in any gift box. No ribbon should be long enough to stretch around it. It is unlimited, all-powerful, and exceedingly abundant. He gives to everyone a measure of faith. Our Father desires to see this gift in action over and over again. You are to offer all your prayers up in faith, believing He hears your cries and will answer.

By using the gift of faith, you can have security in the Father. When you step out in faith and see God work, you find security knowing He is present. You can be as secure in your relationship with Him as you want to be. He offers you the assurance of being one of His children and wants you to return the security in Him as your Father. He wants His name stamped all over you. He wants His name to stand forth in your deeds and actions. "Whether, then, you eat or drink or whatever you do, do all to the glory of God" (1 Cor. 10:31, NASB). Is your Father glorified in all you do?

He wants you to say, "I am (insert your name), son/daughter of the King of kings and Lord of lords; I am (insert your name), a child of the Messiah; I am (insert your name), son/daughter of the Living God; I am (insert your name), child of the Prince of Peace and the Lamb of Glory!"

Hallelujah! I get chills up and down my spine just writing it because I feel it deep within my soul. The Heavenly Father loves it when we can give back to Him this gift of security. He loves it when you call Him Daddy. If you do not regularly claim your Father, how can you ever claim your inheritance?

God will protect you and keep you in perfect peace. "The steadfast of mind You will keep in perfect peace, because he trusts in You" (Isa. 26:3, NASB). He will protect you from the enemy. He will always give you a way out of the devil's snares. "Therefore let him who thinks he stands take heed that he does not fall. No temptation has overtaken you but such as is common to man; and God is faithful, who will not allow you to be tempted beyond what you are able, but with the temptation provide the way to escape also, so that you will be able to endure it" (1 Cor. 10:12–13, NASB).

The question is this: Will you give God the same protection in return? Will you show Him that you protect yourself? Do you prevent yourself from going places you should not go and from looking at things you should not look at? Do you refrain from feeding your mind on negative and ungodly thoughts? Do you avoid situations that tempt you to sin? Are you truly showing the Heavenly Father that you take purposeful steps to protect yourself from sin? If not, you need to find ways to show your Father this gift of protection.

One major way to protect yourself is to follow the Father's guidance. If you fail to follow His guidance, the Father offers forgiveness. He forgives everything you have ever done if you only ask. He sent his first and only Son, Jesus Christ, to die on the cross and shed His blood for your sins—and yet many times you cannot forgive others. Practice forgiveness, and forgive those who have hurt you. You are commanded to forgive one another as Christ has forgiven you. "For if you forgive others for their transgressions, your Heavenly Father will also forgive you" (Matt. 6:14, NASB). So get busy! Start cleaning from your heart that unforgiving spirit and get freedom! You will be forgiven in the same manner in which you forgive others. Doesn't that scare you if you are holding something against someone? Do you want to live with the feeling that your Father does not forgive you?

Let your Father see the gift of forgiveness in you. This is pleasing to Him. He does not want you carrying the baggage that weighs you down by not forgiving. He wants you to find freedom to forgive as you are forgiven. Show God you forgive yourself as well. If the all-loving Father can forgive you, let it go and forgive yourself. Do not ponder sins of the past nor let the devil rob you of the joy of knowing you are forgiven. "As far as the east is from the west, So far has He removed our transgressions from us" (Ps. 103:12, NASB). Your sins are as far as the east is from the west, and they are remembered no more—they are washed by the blood of the Lamb. Praise God! Hallelujah!

When you break the relationship with God the Father, He is ready to restore you. If you seek the face of God and confess your broken relationship, He will begin to embrace you in His arms once again. "I will give them a heart to know me, for I am the Lord; and they will be my people, and I will be their God, for they will return to Me with their whole heart" (Jer. 24:7, NASB). God wants you to return to Him with your whole heart, and He *will* hear you. He will transform our hearts to know Him, and yet we cannot restore our broken relationships with the people in our lives. God is not pleased when you leave broken relationships shattered. He wants you to mend, heal, and allow others to be healed and restore relationships. He wants to see restoration operating in your life. Are you willing to restore your relationship with Him if it is not where it should be? Will you be willing to take steps to restore relationships lost with others?

Restoring your relationship with God allows Him to start a transformation process in your life. Let the Father see your willingness to come to Him and ask Him to transform your heart, mind, and soul. Allow Him to transform you from the inside out. He needs to start in the inner court, transforming your heart to a heart like His, transforming your eyes to focus on Him, transforming your ears to hear His voice, and transforming your mind into the mind of Christ. He wants to transform your lips to only speak words of encouragement and edification, transform your hands to be willing to reach out to embrace and help others, and transform your feet to walk the path of righteousness. Once your life has been transformed, show thanks to the Heavenly Father for what He has done in your life by sharing every part that he has transformed with others. Be a part of helping others be transformed. Don't keep the love of the Father a secret.

Two days before typing about restoration, I had the most beautiful opportunity to see it in action. I know a man who is losing all use of his muscles from a rare disease. As he lies in bed day after day, God has been going through the transformation process with him. He and his daughter had a broken relationship since the day he had separated from her mother. She was only seven years of age at the time of separation. Hurt and pain had festered for over thirty-five years. Dad was not present at many of her events while growing up. Family members told her lies, adding to her confusion. She felt her father left her as well. And she never felt loved and accepted by her stepmother. They had seen each other, but the relationship was a strain. I had been praying for months for this relationship to be restored.

I had the opportunity to meet his daughter about four months prior to the healing taking place, and we had become friends as well. I received a call from her, asking if I had time to talk with her. We met the same afternoon, and through brokenness, hurt, and pain, she was willing to go to her father and try to mend the relationship. We prayed together and went to see him, trusting the Lord for a healing to take place and the process of restoration to begin. After the father and daughter talked together and poured out their hearts, I wept when I heard this father say to his daughter, "The most beautiful thing that came out of all the pain in marriage and divorce to your mother was you." Then later I could see in his eyes the desire to get up out of the bed that bound him when he said, "If I could get out of this bed, crawl on my hands and knees, and rest at your feet to tell you how sorry I am, I would."

These were priceless words. Then the picture I received in my mind was of Jesus Christ saying, "With all the pain I went through when I was mocked, stripped, stabbed in the head with a crown of thorns, beaten, and then pierced with nails in My hands and feet and left to hang on the cross, it was all worth if just for you." I cannot even type it without coming to tears. And, yes, He was willing to die and come out of that grave and return to the Father just so we could be forgiven. He was willing to plead with the Father to "forgive them, for they know not what they do" (Luke. 23:34, NASB).

Within seconds, I saw this beautiful young lady crawl up on her daddy's bed, lay her head on his shoulders, wrap her arms around his neck, and just sob. The words "I love you" went back and forth many times, and I praised God and left them to spend time together in each other's arms. I know her daddy could not physically even pick up his arms and wrap them around her, but I can assure you his daughter felt them.

Isn't this just like the Father? He is always willing to tell you He loves you. He is always willing to hold you in His arms and comfort you. He is always willing to restore your relationship with Him or start a new relationship if you are only willing. Just like this lovely young lady with her dad, we have to start by coming to Him. He can never have too many children. He is preparing a mansion with enough rooms for everyone who will come. He has a seat for you at His banquet table. Isn't that just like a daddy?

Bring forth your life as a vessel. Make yourself a living sacrifice for Him. Yield to Him as He draws near to you. Let God become the Father He wants to be to you. Take every gift He offers you, and delight in it, share it, and return it to Him. Use it with diligence. You can *never* wear it out.

My prayer for all readers is this:

> Father, may Your kingdom come and Your will be done—on earth and in the life of everyone who reads this today. May we all be drawn to spread our wings like eagles and soar to the mountaintop, where we can be drawn closer and closer to You. Help us to know You like You know us—personally and intimately. Help each of us to seek to be holy before You. May our hearts, minds, and souls be revived for You—ready to plunge forward and do our part to complete the body of Christ right here on earth. Help us to realize we are all vessels for You and that You want to fill us until we are running over—running over and pouring out on to all those around us. Give us bold hearts for You, Lord, so we are not afraid to speak out for You and tell others how wonderful You are. You are the greatest, dear Father, and we love You and give You all the praise and glory for all that You are going to do in the lives of people willing to be Your children. Amen.

Study Questions

Are you ready to trust Him with your life?

Can God trust you with no conditions attached?

How faithful are you to God? Do you need to be more faithful?

Are you secure in your relationship with God, or do you sometimes doubt your salvation?

Is God glorified in all you do? What areas of your life need to be changed?

Do you take steps to protect yourself from sin? If so, how do you protect yourself? What steps do you need to take to protect yourself from falling into sin in areas where you may be weak?

CPSIA information can be obtained
at www.ICGtesting.com
Printed in the USA
LVOW04s0746190816
500924LV00005B/27/P